CONDITIONING YOUR MIND

TO FUEL Creativity

BY JENNIFER YAROS

SMART BUSINESS® BOOKS
An Imprint of Smart Business® Network Inc.

Published by:
Smart Business Network
835 Sharon Drive, Suite 200
Westlake, OH 44145

Printed in the United States of America
Editor: Dustin S. Klein

ISBN: 978-1-945389-69-6
Library of Congress Control Number: 2018950920

Printed in USA

ACKNOWLEDGEMENTS

I would like to express my gratitude to my boss, Angie, who saw the potential of my crazy idea and paved the way to make it a reality. Without her backing BrainSpark and this book would not exist.

To Ginny for being the other half of my brain and my reality check. Your advice and feedback were invaluable.

To Ray for listening to my excited babble and for being a sounding board during long runs on the trails. Your support and encouragement gave me courage when I doubted myself and felt overwhelmed.

Thank you to my daughter, Miranda for being patient and never complaining. You are an amazingly beautiful and self-sufficient young woman.

Finally, and most importantly, to my mom, Sandy. Thank you for teaching me to dream, to fight for what I want, and to never stop reaching for the stars.

CONTENTS

I. THE CREATIVE PROCESS 7
   Creativity vs Innovation 8
   What is Creativity? 10
   Why is Creativity Important? 12
   Who is Creative? 14
   The Science Behind Creativity 16
      1. Parts of the Brain...17
      2. Chemical Reactions in the Brain 23
   How Do You Learn to be Creative? 25

II. PREPARE YOUR BODY AND SENSES....................................33
   Promoting a Creative State of Mind....................................34
      1. Silence Your Monkey Brain 35
      2. Energize with Exercise 39
      3. Set Your Personal Space 41
      4. Laughter is the Best Medicine 43
   You Have Five Senses, Use Them All 46
      1. Let Your Nose Lead the Way....................................... 48
      2. All I Need is This Fuzzy Blanket, and This Paddleball Game........... 49
      3. Really See What is Around You....................................50
      4. Stimulate Your Taste Buds 52
      5. Coffee Shops—Skip the Coffee and Go for the Noise 53

III. PREPARE YOUR THINKING.. 57
   Warp Your Mind 59
      1. Be Child-like 60
      2. Practice Divergent Thinking 65
      3. Flip Your Questions, Flip Your Perspective.................. 69
   Get More Inputs 75
      1. How Multiple Inputs Expand Creativity.......................76
      2. Be Curious. Ask Questions..77
      3. Be Courageous. Try Something New 81
   Become Idea Prone 84
      1. Don't Overthink 85
      2. Transitioning Between Left and Right 86
      3. Improve Upon Existing 91

CONTENTS

Recognize Interconnections 93
   1. Look to Nature—Biomimcry............................ 95
   2. Unusual Connections—Bislocation 96
   3. Make the Old New Again............................... 98

IV. PREPARE YOUR EGO 101
Fail... Like a Genius™..102
   1. Embrace Failure 104
   2. Learn From Failures 106
   3. Reassess Failure 107
Deal With Constraints 109
   1. Detour Down the Path Less Traveled...............109
   2. Reimagine Your Environment 112
Learn to Use Collaboration and Competition 114

V. QUICK HITS TO FLIP THE CREATIVITY SWITCH...............119
Inspirations..119
   1. Advice from Experts 119
   2. Standup and Stretch 121
   3. Look on the Internet 121
   4. Mind Map or Draw a Picture 121
   5. Exercise 122
   6. Meditate and Breathe 122
   7. Memory or Vision Boards 122
   8. Share 122
Activities 123
   1. A Bit of Everything Activity............................123
   2. 20 Circles Activity.....................................124
   3. Height Challenge 127
Toolbox 128
   1. Be Prepared 128
   2. Hand Toys and Wake-up Bags™ 129
   3. Post-It® Notes...131
   4. Idea Journal 131

THE CREATIVE PROCESS

PART I

CLOSE YOUR EYES. YES, I UNDERSTAND THE IRONY OF AN AUTHOR TELLING THAT TO A READER, BUT HUMOR ME. CLOSE YOUR EYES FOR 20 SECONDS AND IMAGINE CREATIVITY.

What picture came to mind?

Was it an odd-looking person with paint smears on his face and clothes, wearing a beret and holding a paint brush in one hand and a pallet in the other?

Or, did you picture a sculpture titled "Summer" but looks like twisted metal with no rhyme or reason?

Maybe you pictured your child's crayon drawing hanging on your refrigerator.

Would you believe that when you have finished reading this book, when I ask you to picture creativity, you will envision the engineer who tells jokes in base-14 (don't ask me to explain, I don't get it either)? You may even see in your mind's eye the programmer with the pocket protector. Or… better yet, you will picture yourself!

That's correct. By the time you have completed this book, you will believe you are creative. Even if you failed high school art class and your children turn your tree upside down during Pictionary to guess what it is, you will feel creative.

Before you ask, no, this book is not going to teach you how to draw, but it will teach you how and why creativity is much more than paint and crayons. Creativity goes beyond creating pictures, building sculptures, and making crafts used for decoration. In the pages that follow, I will break down your preconceptions about what creativity is and means, and rebuild an image of it with you at the center.

First, let me explain the difference between artistic and creative. Being "artistic" means you have the skills and ability to create paints, draw, sculpt, compose, write, etc. Being "creative" means you generate ideas and use your imagination to create ways to solve problems.

Creativity, at its most basic level, is a set of ideas which leads to something new. Creativity spurs innovation. It is used to better a company's products, services, and processes. Creativity is what separates companies that are just "in business" with those that excel.

Throughout history, many of the people we remember best are those who demonstrated their innovative ideas and ability to apply creativity to problem-solving. These people motivate and inspire us. They leave indelible imprints on everything they touch.

What's more, a person can even be a creative speaker. Yes, creativity can be found in any form and any medium—speech, writing, thoughts; as well as those things you'd typically associate with creativity—paints, clay, metal, and photographs. My goal is to prove this to you.

Whew!

That's quite a challenge I've set for myself in writing this book: Not only will I prove that you can be creative, but I'll also provide a set of tools you can use to develop your creativity and solve everyday problems. It's a toolkit useful for developing your own team of creative people who can band together to solve business problems and put your organization on the leading edge of today's quickly advancing innovation-driven marketplace.

Creativity vs Innovation

At first blush, there may not seem to be much daylight between creativity and innovation. After all, I laid out the correlation between the two earlier, saying that creativity spurs innovation. Some people use the two terms interchangeably, but they are very different.

Creativity is the method of unleashing the mind to think in different ways and imagine new ideas. Creativity does not have a measurable outcome.

Innovation, on the other hand, is the application of creativity. It introduces change to a system or product, and is the process required to make that change. Innovation does have a measurable result.

Often, a creative idea results in an innovative product or process, which in turn provides a company with a measurable return on investment. However, not all creativity will lead to innovation, and not all innovation is profitable.

Confused?

Let me illustrate with a story: Pixar, the animation powerhouse, was once a little company struggling to remain alive. It had an **innovative** imaging marvel called the Pixar Image Computer. This machine rendered 2D images into 3D images, which at the time was amazing.

The little company had a dream to create a feature-length animated film to demonstrate its innovation, but it lacked the revenue to fund this dream.

So, the leaders of this Oliver Twist of companies devised a **creative** idea: they would market the Pixar Image Computer to industries other than animation. Pixar applied this **creative** idea, which lead to the **innovative** process of seeking buyers from government and medical agencies. These industries could use the machine to turn CT images into 3D images, making them easier to read.

Eventually, the company caught the eye of Steve Jobs, who saw its potential and helped fund the company so it could realize the animation dreams.

Everyone knows how this story ends: Pixar has animated many award-winning films and today is one of the top creative and innovative companies in the world. But, it was the initial **innovative** product coupled with the **innovative** application of the **creative** funding idea that set the company on the path to where it is today. Simply put: Creative Ideas → Innovative Products or Processes → ROI.

What is Creativity?

While doing research for this book, I surveyed creative people from different industries. My first question was "How do you define creativity?" I expected to receive a lot of responses about making something out of nothing or improving something already in existence. After all, that's how the books I read defined creativity. The answers I received, however, were as varied as the people with whom I spoke. Granted, there were reoccurring themes which danced around the standard definition, but the most common words were divergent, thought-provoking, different, ideas, perspective, experiment, problem-solving, and solution.

One response stood out for both its elegance and the complexity of the response. It not only answers "What is creativity," but also touches on other topics, into which I will delve later.

Jason Walker, a UX Designer from Colorado, replied: *"Creativity is a cornerstone of humanity... I think it exists in different stages and evolves from instinct to skill over the course of a lifetime... it can be strengthened or it can be allowed to atrophy."*

He continued, *"I think it starts off as a survival instinct, a mechanism for early learning and early problem solving. At this stage, it is unbridled by additional knowledge and the fear of failure that often accompanies knowledge. If creativity is nurtured through divergent learning activities, it grows and strengthens into a refined skill... if it is stifled through a routine of consistent, unyielding convergent-learning it withers.*

"Creativity is a type of fearlessness, to take chances, to experiment, to question and formulate potential solutions. It's the first half of the design process, unencumbered by a fear of failure or a desire for result."

Let's look closer at Walker's definition.

First, he calls it the "cornerstone of humanity." Does he mean that the crude drawings on cave walls were essential to the human species' survival and evolution? No. I don't think so. Rather, I think Walker means that it took creative thinking for early man to survive and evolve into the technological beast of today.

Using this line of thinking, creativity can be found in the ways cavemen figured out how to live in cold climates and find food. Creativity played a role in how they developed tools and evolved society. Creativity, under this scenario, is a mindset and a way of thinking. The product of creativity therefore can be found in the art, tools, solutions, and innovations.

Another observation Walker makes is that creativity is not a talent only some people are born with. He asserts that it exists in everyone initially as an instinct, but the people who nurture and develop it learn to use it to solve complex problems. Creativity becomes a powerful skill in their personal toolbox. Let me say that again: <u>Creativity is not a talent that some are born with; it is an innate skill everyone has, and those who consciously work to develop it are our innovators.</u>

Does this mean anyone can learn to use creativity to develop innovative solutions to problems?

The answer is a resounding "YES!"

This brings us full circle to the focus of the book you hold in your hands: to provide you with the creative toolbox to develop what already exists within you.

As part of the goal to "show" you how to do this rather than simply "tell" you, I've offered several divergent learning activities, which will help strengthen and condition your mind to think creatively. Not all activities or methods will work for everyone, but there is at least one within these pages which will help every reader nurture and grow his or her creativity.

Conversely, as there are ways to develop creativity, there are always ways to crush it like a wrecking ball. You'll learn about some of those hazards and how to avoid them, or, just as important, how to make them work for you instead of against you.

As for Walker, he astutely identified the biggest creativity crusher of them all: fear of failure. Accordingly, there is an entire section of this book devoted to learning how to embrace failure instead of fearing it. By doing so, you'll start to Fail... Like a Genius™.

Another enemy of creativity is laziness. It requires time, energy, and—I'm sorry to say—the dreaded "W" word, work, to tap into and use creativity. While it's true that everyone has it inside himself, it requires work to fully develop and use it. As Thomas Edison said, "Opportunity is missed by many because it wears overalls and looks like work." Or, as the NHL hockey legend Wayne Gretzky once mused, "You miss 100 percent of the shots you never take."

Why is Creativity Important?

A study conducted at the Santa Fe Institute in New Mexico determined that publicly-traded companies have an average lifespan of 10 years. It found their usual method of death comes about through acquisitions, mergers, or bankruptcies. Historically speaking, the World Economic Forum found that of today's Fortune 500 companies, the average lifespan is somewhere between 40 and 50 years. That said, it's worth noting that of the 500 companies that appeared on the Forbes list back in 1999, half of them were gone within 10 years, and every year that percentage worsens. A study from the John M. Olin School of Business at Washington University estimates that three out of four of today's Fortune 500 companies on the S&P 500 will no longer exist in 2027. Whichever way you read the numbers, it's become apparent that the days when it was assumed companies would last for generations and be passed down from one family member to the next, have become more of the exception rather than the norm.

So, what is happening to our companies today where those that appear strong at one moment are at risk of survival in the next?

Complacency.

Sure, we've all heard the saying, "If it's not broke, don't fix it." When it comes to business, however, and certainly where creativity comes into play, it's not good advice.

Consider Kodak, the former No. 1 photography company in the world. It developed the first digital camera in 1975, created a sensor with 1.4 million pixels by 1986, yet never fully embraced the idea of digital photography. As we all know, Kodak ended up being caught with its pants down by the time the digital age elbowed its way into the photography business, and the company paid a steep price.

More broadly speaking, the United States continues to use the same business models and same education practices that have been used for decades. Many companies in the private sector tend to ride the coattails of one big product for too long before they start to look for their next big thing. As Kyung Hee Kim, a professor of innovation and creativity at the College of William & Mary found, it's a problem of epic proportions.

Kim studied the results of 300,000 Torrance Tests of Creative Thinking taken by people from kindergarten age to adulthood between 1968 and 2008, and came to a startling—and disturbing—conclusion. While IQ tests have been on the rise, since 1990, the Torrance scores have been in steady decline. So, while we are getting smarter as a people, we're becoming less creative.

This has been happening during a time in history when other countries have stepped up their competition against the U.S. While we've been focused on other things, other nations have taken a hard look at how the U.S. operates and begun asking, "How can we do that... but better?"

This is the type of creative thinking that leads to innovation, and while the U.S. has either remained stagnant or declined a bit—depending on your viewpoint of things—other countries have closed the gap and some have already caught up. Several of them have not only improved on U.S. practices, but they have also acknowledged the importance of creative thinking as it relates to economic growth. These countries are incorporating creativity into the schools as part of standard curriculum, and now teach the next generation how to use creativity to solve problems for business, industry, and government.

As a result, these nations have restructured the way knowledge is transferred to students, pivoting from the U.S. standard practice of having a single teacher lead a classroom of approximately 25 students through a lecture on a single subject for about an hour.

Stagnation has contributed to the U.S. losing its creative and innovative edge, and as a result, American companies are finding it more difficult to compete in the global market against countries that are committed to evolving and improving. Those that remain powerhouses are the ones already researching and developing new products and services at the same time their current "big products and services" are hitting the market.

According to a poll of 1,500 CEOs by IBM, the No. 1 leadership competency of the future is creativity.

Further, there's more than just economic growth at stake. All around us are issues crying out for creative solutions: Life in the oceans are dying at an alarming rate. People in Third World countries need clean water. Healthcare remains unaffordable for millions of people. Jails are overpopulated. There isn't a cure for ALS.

UX Designer Jason Walker explains the importance of creativity this way: "Design and innovation are driven by creativity. Without either, the human condition does not advance. We become incapable of dreaming up the solutions that make life better for our fellow man. Major world problems become incapable of being solved."

Think about smartphones, four-wheel drive, airbags, rapid response emergency systems, and recycling. None of these would exist without the minds of people who saw a problem and creatively found an innovative solution.

Who is Creative?

In 1997, Apple released its "Think Different" manifesto. The manifesto best explains who is considered creative:

Here's to the crazy ones. The misfits. The rebels. The round pegs in the square holes. Those ones who see things differently... Because they change things. They invent. They imagine. They heal. They explore. They create. They inspire. They push the human race forward...

Creative people, as Apple insists, are not just artists, musicians, or writers. Creative people include scientists, engineers, strategists, and yes, even every day, ordinary people. You are a creative person.

Still skeptical?

Consider this: Do you ever daydream about what you want to do when you retire? Have you ever considered a process that has been used for years in your office and mused, "I know a more efficient way to do this?" Do you ever do something, and then think of an idea which would make the task easier or automate it? What about spontaneously humming a tune? If you answered "yes" to any of these questions, then you, my friend, are creative.

Let's look at it another way. I like lists. Sometimes, they are the best way to get a point across. Each year, Fast Company and Inc. magazine publish on their respective websites the 100 most creative people in industry and business. A close look reveals that creativity can be found anywhere. Here's just a sampling of the industries where top creative people belong:

- Design
- Diversity and education
- Entertainment
- Fashion and beauty
- Finance and commerce
- Food
- Music
- Science and health
- Social good
- Sports
- Tech
- Transportation

This list is not all-inclusive, so just because you are an accountant is not a good reason to think creativity does not apply to you—just stay away from "creative" accounting, if you get my drift. The reality is that creativity affects everyone and every industry, including politics and the military. If you don't believe me, you have obviously not listened to recent political campaigns or planned a battle strategy in the game Axis & Allies. There is a bit of creativity in everyone.

Famously creative people—the ones everyone has heard of—are those who work on it constantly and develop their creativity like a muscle. The late author Ray Bradbury is just one example. Bradbury, a prolific writer, authored books, short stories, screenplays, and television scripts. He wrote seven days a week, and produced 30 short stories each year. His most famous works were the *Martian Chronicles* and *Fahrenheit 451*.

Was everything Bradbury wrote perfect, or even published? No. But the act of observing the events and items around him, and using those as inspirations to craft stories, became a constant exercise in creativity. It brings to mind the old joke: How do you get to Carnegie Hall?

PRACTICE!

As with anything else, there are many ways to practice creativity. Not every method works for every person. Like tennis, some people learn best by getting out onto the court and immediately swinging the racket. They learn the rules and proper form by doing. Others learn best by reading the rules and watching how to serve a tennis ball on YouTube before picking up a racket.

The key is to find the methods that work best for you and start practicing. Relentlessly. On the pages that follow, you'll find different methods for practicing—and unleashing—your creativity. Who knows, maybe you'll learn new ways to develop it to your full potential. But it's up to you to give it a try and find the methods that work, and then commit to doing them daily.

The Science Behind Creativity

The world-famous astronomer, cosmologist, astrophysicist, astrobiologist, author, science popularizer, and science communicator Carl Sagan built a legacy on his ability to combine the power of creativity with the natural laws of science. He once said, "It is the tension between creativity and skepticism that has produced the stunning and unexpected findings of science."

Nearly a century earlier, American philosopher and education reformer

John Dewey, long considered one of the fathers of functional psychology, noted, "Every great advance in science has issued from a new audacity of the imagination."

And Willis Harman and Howard Rheingold observed in their 1984 bestselling book *Higher Creativity*, "While the rational mind is important, we gain a new perspective when we learn how many of the greatest scientific insights, discoveries, and revolutionary inventions appeared first to their creators as fantasies, dreams, trances, lightening-flash insights, and other non-ordinary states of consciousness."

So, what do these great thinkers have in common?

Simply put, they all recognized the symbiotic relationship between creativity and science: it all comes down to understanding the brain.

1. Parts of the Brain

Have you ever taken a test that reveals which side of your brain you use more—the left or right? The test relies on a series of questions to evaluate if you are more of an analytical thinker (left side) or a more creative type (right side).

These tests often show I evenly use my right and left brain, which made me wonder if it was better to be evenly distributed. There's a commonly held notion that artist-types should be more right brain oriented and engineers or people who work with numbers should be more left brain oriented.

The truth is, however, whenever you have a problem that is not easily solvable, you use both sides of your brain. So regardless of your profession, it is smart to work on developing your entire brain—left and right.

Think of a time when you used brainstorming to solve a problem. If you're like me, the first few minutes are such that you have so many ideas that it becomes difficult to write them down fast enough. Eventually, the flow of ideas slows… and then stops.

As you stare at the paper, tapping your foot and chewing on your pencil, you suddenly have an idea. It's completely different than any other idea you've had, and you believe it is a stroke of genius.

This is your left and right brain at work.

One of the best ways to illustrate this is to paint an image of how the left and right hemispheres of the brain work together to solve problems:

Mr. Left Brain is like the loud-mouthed, co-worker who knows everything about anything. This is the man who has been at the company forever and thinks there is nothing he has not witnessed. He has all the answers.

Alternately, Mr. Right Brain is the fresh-faced, college-graduate, new hire who is eager to put into practice what he's learned from his liberal arts education.

One day, the owner of the food manufacturing company where they work presents both men with an issue: The byproduct of their pickle-making process is costing the company too much money. The owner wants Mr. Left Brain and Mr. Right Brain to develop solutions for reducing the cost of disposing of the food by-product.

Mr. Left Brain immediately walks to the white board and in a loud, booming voice rattles off ideas, barely taking a breath between explaining each idea. Within five minutes, Mr. Left Brain has 20 ideas written on the whiteboard. Each solution is very practical, if somewhat obvious, such as researching disposal companies for cheaper rates.

After Mr. Left Brain's quick recitation of ideas, he sits down, quite pleased with himself, thinking there could not possibly be any more ideas.

During this break in the mad rush of ideas, Mr. Right Brain decides he can finally speak and stands up to add his ideas to the board.

While Mr. Left Brain was busy spouting obvious answers to the problem, Mr. Right Brain was quietly contemplating alternate, less obvious, solutions by using the ideas Mr. Left Brain recommended as starting points. As a result, the new ideas Mr. Right Brain adds to the board are creative and different. Sure, some are impractical, but others have enough merit that they are worth exploring further. For example, instead of disposing of the brine, why doesn't the company make a new food product out of it, such as a bloody mary mix? Now instead of one product they would have two and less waste.

What this scenario demonstrates is that different types of solutions require different approaches to thinking. That's because the left hemisphere of your brain is where the logical connections are stored. Every solution to problems you've already encountered is readily available there. The initial burst of ideas you have about a problem come from the left side of the brain because it's filled with low-hanging fruit.

But once those logical solutions are exhausted and your left brain quiets, it's time for your right brain to kick in and offer solutions it has been mulling over quietly in the background. This is also known as inspiration. The ideas seem to suddenly come out of thin air and are less obvious—or, as the entomology of the word "inspiration" suggests, the ideas come from divine guidance.

Have you ever experienced a moment of inspiration while in the shower or in the dead of night? This is where those ideas come from.

One suggestion: If you are ever stuck on an idea, try walking away from it and giving your left brain a break. Your right brain may soon jump into the void when your thoughts are elsewhere and provide you with a solution.

And here's a fun tip to ensure you don't lose those awesome shower ideas: Keep a whiteboard marker in the bathroom. Write down your ideas on the mirror until you get to a piece of paper and a pen.

ACTIVITIES

LEFT BRAIN / RIGHT BRAIN

Just like creativity, anyone can develop and sharpen left brain/right brain problem-solving skills. Brain teasers or inspiration puzzles are a perfect way to practice. Here are a few puzzles to get your brain firing on all neurons:*

1 SUICIDE OR NOT?

A man was found dead with a cassette recorder in one hand and a gun in the other.

The police arrived on the scene and immediately pressed the play button on the cassette.

On the recording, the man is heard saying, "I have nothing else to live for. I can't go on," which is followed by the sound of a gunshot.

After listening to the cassette tape, the police knew this was not a suicide, but rather a homicide.

How did they deduce this?

2 SOLVE THIS EQUATION BY MOVING JUST ONE MATCHSTICK.

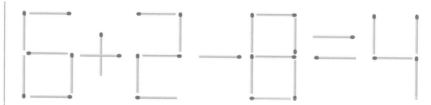

3 **SIMPLE QUERY OR TOUGH QUESTION?**

What always runs, but never walks; often murmurs, never talks; has a bed, but never sleeps; has a mouth, but never eats?

4 **DETERMINE THE MISSING NUMBER.**

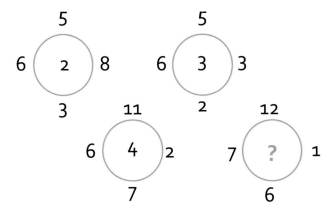

5 **FIND THE POISON.**

Two girls ate dinner together. They both ordered iced tea. One girl drank her iced tea very fast and finished five glasses in the time it took the other girl to drink just one. The girl who drank one glass of iced tea died while the other girl survived. All the drinks were poisoned. How did the girl who drank the most survive?

*ACTIVITY ANSWER KEY ON PAGE 31

ACTIVITIES

6 BONUS!

Author's Note: This puzzle is rumored to have been written by Albert Einstein, and it's been said that 98 percent of people cannot solve it. It is not a difficult puzzle, but does require close attention to detail.

There are five houses in five colors. In each house lives a person with a different nationality. The five owners drink a certain type of beverage, smoke a certain brand of cigar, and keep a certain pet. No owners have the same pet, smoke the same brand of cigar, or drink the same beverage.

The question is: Who owns the fish?

Hints:
The Brit lives in the red house.
The Swede keeps dogs as pets.
The Dane drinks tea.
The green house is on the left of the white house.
The green homeowner drinks coffee.
The person who smokes Pall Mall rears birds.
The owner of the yellow house smokes Dunhill.
The man living in the center house drinks milk.
The Norwegian lives in the first house.
The man who smokes Blend lives next to the one who keeps cats.
The man who keeps the horse lives next to the man who smokes Dunhill.
The owner who smokes Bluemaster drinks beer.
The German smokes Prince.
The Norwegian lives next to the blue house.
The man who smokes Blend has a neighbor who drinks water.

Solution:

Nationality	Norwegian	Dane	Brit	German	Swede
House	Yellow	Blue	Red	Green	White
Animal	Cats	Horses	Birds	Fish	Dogs
Cigar	Dunhill	Blend	Pall Mall	Prince	Bluemaster
Drink	Water	Tea	Milk	Coffee	Beer

You may have been able to quickly and easily answer some of these puzzles because you recognized them. However, this type of thought is not due to reactions in either your right or left brain. Rather, let's introduce another part of the brain into the equation: the frontal lobe.

While the left hemisphere of the brain is the logical, analytical side and the right hemisphere is the creative side, the frontal lobe is responsible for memories. The more times you encounter something, and the more similar connections you make, the more likely it will be added to your memory and thus more easily recalled.

The frontal lobe is also responsible for intense concentration. This is extremely helpful after you experience a moment of inspiration so you can work on perfecting your solution.

2. Chemical Reactions in the Brain

Want more science? You got it! Let's get technical and explore chemical reactions in the brain.

Noted neuroeconomist and professor Baba Shiv wrote about chemical reactions in *Stanford Business*: "The right neurochemical cocktail for your best creative work is a high level of both serotonin and dopamine," he said. "This will produce a condition in which you are calm but energized."

Serotonin and dopamine are neurotransmitters. Serotonin helps regulate your mood while dopamine controls the brain's pleasure and reward system.

Another neurotransmitter that helps with creative thinking is endorphins. Endorphins combat anxiety and stress leaving your mind calm and open for new ideas.

When you have healthy levels of serotonin, endorphins, and dopamine, you feel excited, enthusiastic, and encouraged. In these moments, the right hemisphere of the brain is more active, so you are more likely to have moments of inspiration.

This moment of inspiration also creates a readable reaction. Scientists discovered that approximately eight seconds before inspiration occurs in a person, alpha waves appear in the right hemisphere of the brain.

There's an opposite chemical reaction as well. Cortisol, a hormone, which inhibits creativity. It is released when we are afraid or stressed, and it is also known as a fight-or-flight hormone. Cortisol is a remainder from our caveman days, when we needed a burst of energy to escape predators. It works in conjunction with two other stress hormones released by the adrenal glands—adrenaline and norepinephrine.

That said, when faced with an issue at work that demands a good solution, you'll never get a raise by running away. To avoid the fight-or-flight response, learn how to practice problem solving. This way, you're able to tap into your left and right brain when necessary—and push fear to the side.

Other creativity inhibitors include stimulants—yes, that coffee mug in your hand may be holding your best creativity at bay. Often, when we are on a tight deadline or have an emergency to quickly resolve, we drink coffee or other caffeinated drinks in attempts to wake up our brain.

However, when you need the help of the creative side of your brain, caffeine and other stimulants, like Adderall, should be low on your list. While these stimulants do exactly what you think they might—help your brain concentrate and focus—they're activating your frontal lobe instead of your creativity centers.

Left Brain Vs. **Right Brain**

Left brain **Right brain**

Right side of body control
- Number skills
- Math/Scientific skills
- Written language
- Spoken language
- Objectivity
- Analytical
- Logic
- Reasoning

Left side of body control
- 3D shapes
- Music/Art awareness
- Intuition
- Creativity
- Imagination
- Subjectivity
- Synthesizing
- Emotion
- Face recognition

The best approach to consider is simply to give your left brain a chance to pick up the problem. Let it fire off all the low-hanging fruit at its disposal and then, when it exhausts every logical idea, take a break. Yes, take a break. Go for a walk, lift weights, read a book, or do something else that makes you happy. Make your body produce serotonin, endorphins, and dopamine by being in a calm, relaxed, and happy state of mind. Once those high alpha waves hit, and you have your moment of inspiration, settle down only at this point with your cup of joe to focus on your idea and perfect it.

As you can see, creativity is not a willy-nilly concept. Inspiration isn't luck. There is a science and process behind it. Any businessperson—engineer, scientist, mathematician, or other supposed "non-creative-type"—can appreciate this. In fact, innovative companies such as 3M and Google encourage employees to take breaks, go for walks, play ping-pong, and even take naps. They recognize the need for people to step away from moments of intense focus so they're able to find inspiration.

How Do You Learn to be Creative?

To develop your creativity, you need to condition your mind to think creatively and generate ideas. Throughout the pages of this book, I approach conditioning your mind in the same way I condition for a 100-mile race. To finish an ultramarathon, it takes more than simply running a lot. I strength

ACTIVITY

INSPIRATION

Imagine for a moment you are opening a new restaurant.

This restaurant is a family-oriented, sit-down diner with a fun atmosphere. Now, you need to write your menu.

Set a timer for five minutes. Write as many menu items as you can during this time. Do not stop until the full five minutes is over.

Oh, and one important fact to keep in mind: your restaurant exists in prehistoric times. Your patrons are cavemen.

By the way, you cannot use the excuse that cavemen can't read, so it doesn't matter what is on the menu. While a creative answer, that's not an acceptable approach. We're pretending and developing our creative thinking.

Ready.
Set.
GO!

After your five minutes have expired, look at your menu items. How many ideas did you generate? How did the flow of ideas occur? Did you notice that initially you wrote a lot and then it tapered out? Did you experience a period where you struggled trying to think of more ideas? Did more ideas eventually come to mind?

Compare the ideas you initially wrote down with those you generated later in the exercise. Did you notice any difference between those which are low-hanging fruit and those which are more unique and creative?

train with weights so my core and upper body are as strong as my legs. I eat a balanced diet so my body is properly fueled. I also practice running in difficult situations such as through cold, fatigue, and mud so I am mentally prepared for the challenges of the race.

In similar fashion, you can learn to condition your mind to think creativity by preparing your body and senses, preparing your thinking, and preparing your ego. Each of these aspects is important for creative thinking and generating ideas. The exercises and tools offered here should serve as your training tools. They are only effective if you use them and practice them. Remember, creativity is a skill which needs to be continuously used and practiced for it to grow and improve. If you take this to heart, you will find that you'll become confident in your ability to use your creativity to solve problems. As a result, you will approach challenges with a different perspective, unique solutions, and innovative ideas.

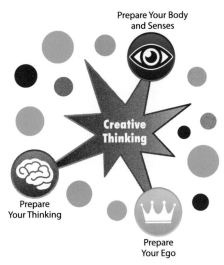

Creativity Assessment

Following is a Creativity Assessment to gauge your current creative proficiency in several areas. Check the Yes box for statements which are true and check No for statements which are false. When you are done, total your Yes responses and then total your No responses. Read the results and then refer to the comparison chart to see which sections of this book you should pay extra attention to.

#	CREATIVITY STATEMENT	YES	NO
1	I take adequate time for contemplation and reflection.		
2	I mediate or pray regularly.		
3	I regularly journal.		
4	The aesthetics of my surroundings affects my mood.		
5	When I eat I enjoy the smells, colors, and textures as much as the flavors.		
6	Form is as important as function.		
7	I often come up with ideas and solutions when exercising.		
8	I get an adequate amount of sleep.		
9	When I am stuck on a problem I stand up and move (i.e. pacing, go for a walk, do jumping jacks, etc.).		
10	I don't always follow the rules.		
11	I don't accept authoritarian assertions without critical examination.		
12	My thinking often goes in a different direction than other people.		
13	I have a sense of humor and /or facility for producing humor.		
14	Sometimes I am silly and immature.		
15	My ideas occasionally have the capacity for fantasy or imagination.		
16	When I am faced with an important decision, I actively seek out different perspectives.		
17	I know a lot about other cultures and am always learning more.		
18	I am open to feelings and emotions. I show emotional sensitivity.		
19	I have a tolerance for ambiguity.		

#	CREATIVITY STATEMENT	YES	NO
20	The integration of dichotomies (i.e. selfish and unselfish, extroverted and introverted) does not cause me anxiety.		
21	I often make connections between two unrelated things.		
22	I am always learning something new.		
23	My friends would describe me as open-minded and curious.		
24	I am open to new experiences and ideas and not frightened by the unknown.		
25	I am skilled at identifying and solving problems.		
26	I often foresee potential problems before others.		
27	I generate a lot of useful ideas.		
28	I accept and deal with failure – turn the failure into something new, learn from it and make improvements, or persevere and keep trying.		
29	I have a tenacity and lack of inhibition (often spontaneous) in expressing of opinion.		
30	I do not mind sharing credit for an idea.		
31	I am adaptable. I make do with what is at hand to reach goals.		
32	I view obstacles as opportunities.		
33	I don't let minor setbacks stop me from achieving my goals.		
34	I solicit feedback from my friends, relations, and colleagues.		
35	Competition energizes me.		
36	I like to work with a team.		

Totals: Yes _____

No _____

Scoring for Total Yes's:

33 – 36 You are a creativity expert. You could teach me a few things.

29 – 32 You are more creative than most people.

26 – 28 You are pretty creative but have room to improve.

22 – 25 Creativity is not at the forefront of your thoughts.
Make time to work on it going forward.

0 – 21 Creativity has not been your thing in the past,
but you are on the right path by just reading this book.

Comparison Chart:

STATEMENT NUMBERS	CORRESPONDING CHAPTER	PAGE NUMBER
1-3	See chapter Promoting a Creative State of Mind	34
4-6	See chapter You Have Senses, Use Them All	46
7-9	See topic Energize with Exercise	39
10-12	See topic Practice Divergent Thinking	65
13-15	See topic Be Child-like	60
16-18	See topic Flip Your Questions, Flip Your Perspective	69
19-21	See chapter Recognize Interconnections	93
22-24	See chapter Get More Inputs	75
25-27	See chapter Become Idea Prone	84
28-30	See chapter Fail... Like a Genius™	102
31-33	See chapter Deal with Constraints	109
34-36	See chapter Learn to Use Collaboration and Competition	114

ACTIVITY ANSWER KEY

1 **SUICIDE OR NOT?**

Answer: If the man shot himself while recording the tape, how did he rewind the cassette tape?

2 **SOLVE THIS EQUATION BY MOVING JUST ONE MATCHSTICK.**

Answer: Move the matchstick from the top right side of the number 8 to fill the gap in the top right side of the number 6 to create an equation that reads: 8+2-6=4

3 **SIMPLE QUERY OR TOUGH QUESTION?**

Answer: A river

4 **DETERMINE THE MISSING NUMBER.**

Answer: 6

5 **FIND THE POISON.**

Answer: The poison was in the ice cubes, which only melted in the girl's glass who drank her iced tea slowly.

6 **BONUS!**

Answer: The German has the fish.

PREPARE YOUR BODY AND SENSES

THE FIRST STEP FOR CONDITIONING YOUR MIND TO THINK CREATIVELY IS DEVELOPING YOUR BODY AND HONING YOUR SENSES. CREATIVE THINKING REQUIRES USING MORE THAN JUST YOUR BRAIN. BY CONDITIONING YOUR BODY AND SENSES, YOU CAN TAP INTO ONE OF THE MOST CRITICAL-YET-OVERLOOKED ESSENTIALS OF CREATIVE THINKING: ENTERING EVERY SITUATION WITH A CALM MIND, ENERGIZED BODY, HAPPY EMOTIONAL STATE, AND SENSES WELL-TRAINED ENOUGH TO USE SURROUNDING STIMULI AS INSPIRATION.

So how can you learn to harness your thoughts and emotional state? What's necessary to ensure your body is conditioned well enough to promote a creative state of mind? And just what skills does it require to tap into and control your senses?

Let's set the stage.

First, find a comfortable, quiet spot to read.

Next, turn on some calming instrumental music. I like the Focus genre on the Spotify app, but find something that you enjoy.

Now, take a few minutes to concentrate simply on breathing.

Take a deep breath in.

Slowly let it out.

Count to five as you inhale; and another five-count as you exhale.

Close your eyes, if you'd like, and feel your body begin to relax.

Are you feeling relaxed? Good. This is the beginning of preparing your body and senses for creative thinking. From this relaxed state, anything is possible.

Promoting a Creative State of Mind

"Creativity is a wild mind and a disciplined eye."

– Dorothy Parker, American poet and author

"Reaching a 'creative' state of mind thru positive action is considered preferable to waiting for 'inspiration.'"

– Minor White, American photographer and theoretician

"If creative work protects a man against mental illness, it is small wonder that he pursues it with avidity; and even if the state of mind he is seeking to avoid is no more than a mild state of depression or apathy, this still constitutes a cogent reason for engaging in creative work even when it brings no obvious external benefit in its train."

– Anthony Storr, British psychiatrist, psychoanalyst and author

"With the practice of deep meditation, the mind contacts the Bliss Consciousness of the Spirit and becomes more peaceful, happy, creative and powerful. This state of mind enriches all values of material life."

– Maharishi Mahesh Yogi, spiritual guru and founder of the Transcendental Meditation technique

What do the preceding quotes all have in common? They illustrate that being creative isn't simply sitting down and saying, "OK. I'm going to think of something creative now." Being creative requires work, it takes practice, and it depends entirely on having the appropriate state of mind.

Reaching that optimum creative state of mind relates back to the brain's neurotransmitters. You want to do things that promote the development of serotonin, dopamine, and endorphins, and avoid the things that promote the development of cortisol. The more you practice achieving a creative state of mind, the easier it becomes to do it at will.

A few ways to promote a more creative state of mind may include learning to calm your mind, finding an inspirational setting, or exercise. Here are some tips you can practice:

1. Silence Your Monkey Brain

In our fast-paced world, the apparent ability to multitask is a point of pride. Looking exhausted and frazzled have become badges of honor. I say "apparent ability" because no matter what you may believe, you're not really completing more tasks. The only things being achieved are high blood pressure, poor eating habits, and tension headaches.

Add the following to the multitasking mix—24/7 social media, kids involved with multiple activities, endless household chores, and the constant bombardment of information. If you're feeling antsy about all the things you should be working on instead of reading this book, then STOP.

BREATHE.

Count to 10.

Do you feel a little better?

Good.

What just happened is your monkey brain took over. The monkey brain is the portion of our brain that reacts immediately instead of thinking things through. When it takes over, we make mindless decisions. Those can cause serious problems.

Worse, the monkey brain gets easily distracted. It causes you to hop from task to task, sometimes not even completing one task before starting the next.

[Hey, look! Squirrel!]

Creative people often have trouble with their monkey brain taking over. They start on a project and in the middle of that project they get a new idea. Then they start working on that new project. Creative people often have UFOs (UnFinished Objects) because of all the ideas floating around in their head. While the development of endless creative ideas is great, seeing

35

them through to completion is what leads to the innovation part of the process—that measurable result we mentioned earlier.

Unfortunately, allowing our monkey brain to rule is often confused with learning and attention disorders, because they appear similar. I won't jump onto that soapbox in this book, but if you are interested in a quick synopsis, The Creative Mind website (www.thecreativemind.net) posted an excellent article, "ADHD and the Creative Mind."

[Ooohhh, shiny]

Now that you see how the monkey mind works, let's look at how you can combate it. In an online article "Please Meet Your Monkey Mind" by Heidi Hanna (https://www.heidihanna.com/journal/2016/4/13/please-meet-your-monkey-mind), she recommends three tips for combatting the monkey brain—eliminating noise, deep breathing, and regular physical activity.

Eliminate the noise. If your mind is on other things, you cannot focus on identifying solutions or generating ideas. You must first clear the clutter and silence the noise in your head. Tim Ferriss, a popular podcaster and author, calls it "caging the monkey mind." Find a quiet place to sit—away from the TV, phone, or computer. If you can't effectively cage the monkey mind, you'll have trouble focusing or sleeping, and you will be more prone to distraction.

Breathe. Breathing helps to relax your mind and body. It also reduces stress. When we are stressed, we become the dumbest version of ourselves. Stress causes the brain to create the neurotransmitter cortisol, which prohibits creative thinking. Therefore, anything you do to reduce stress, such as taking deep breaths or meditating, helps your creativity flow. Interestingly enough, as I conducted research for this book, I found evidence of the greatest leaders taking time each day to do some type of deep breathing, meditation, or relaxation routine. If you need help relaxing, there is a great app called Breathe+ Relaxation and Breath Training by Dynamic App Design, LLC. It helps you visualize your breathing so you can relax and think clearly.

Try to do a physical activity every 90 minutes. I like to run and to go to the batting cages to take a few swings, but if I can't get out of the office, I switch to my standing desk and play with hand toys. My favorite hand toy is a metal slinky. The feel of the coils combined with the monotonous shling- shling- shling are very soothing. The bottom line: do anything that will get your brain producing dopamine, serotonin, and endorphins.

Beyond these three top-of-mind tips, there are several other activities you can engage in to tame the wild beast of your monkey mind:

- **Focus on the problem at hand.** Try not to multitask.
- **Purge negative and fearful thoughts.** Negativity and fear are just as detrimental to creative thinking as stress.
- **Go outside into the sunlight.** Sunlight increases serotonin levels, which helps put you in a good mood and increases creative thinking.
- **Eat well.** A healthy diet also helps serotonin production.
- **Perform acts of kindness.** Giving and receiving helps to improve your mood. For ideas on different acts of kindness, see Berkley University's Greater Good Center's website (https://ggsc.berkeley.edu/) for their Happiness Calendar. Every month, they release a new calendar with daily acts of kindness you can perform.
- **Get enough sleep.** The brain needs adequate sleep to function properly.
- **Manage your emotions.** Sometimes it is not possible to control how you feel. It is important to know that it is OK to seek help, and that help is out there. Get treatment for depression if you need it.
- **Do something monotonous.** Performing mindless tasks, like doodling or vacuuming, allows your mind to wander.

If all else fails, you can also unplug and hide. This may sound funny. However, while working on this book, I became acutely aware at how disruptive small interruptions are. Every time my inbox chimed, I looked at the pop-up notification. Often, I would open my email and either delete the junk or respond to an actionable email. These small tasks would take me down a rabbit hole of emails, websites, texts, and phone calls. Before I realized it, I would lose an hour of writing time.

Research from Stanford neuroscientists Vinod Menon and Daniel Levitin revealed that the daily noise of text messages, phone calls, TV advertisements, and other stimulation take a toll on our mental state. Unfortunately, we do not have enough mental power to deal with all the noise and still think creatively. The consumption of information does not allow time for our brains to switch to idea generation. Subsequently, we are left feeling overwhelmed and tired.

If you have the flexibility, set aside dedicated creative time. Block your calendar from meetings, turn off every communication device around you, and allow yourself to create… uninterrupted.

Better yet, the next time you feel your mind wandering or feel overwhelmed with tasks piling up around you, throw a banana into a cage. When your monkey brain follows, lock the door.

ACTIVITIES

1 DISCONNECT THE MONKEY BRAIN
Spend an entire day disconnected from anything that can distract you – internet, phone, tv, news, kids, etc. Dedicate the entire day to relaxing. Keep a journal nearby to record any creative ideas that come to mind. If you don't get any ideas, that is okay. You will return to your daily life refreshed and your mind ready for any challenge.

I understand that an entire day disconnected may be scary to some people. Start smaller with a few hours or a half-day. Work your way up to an entire day.

2 **DISCONNECT THE SENSES**

Another idea is to try a sensory deprivation tank or isolation tank. This is a lightless, soundproof tank filled with water. You go inside and float for an hour. Just as your body relaxes and floats, so does your mind.

If that idea terrifies you more than disconnecting for a day, then maybe a silent retreat is a better option for you. This is a way to disconnect, yet you avoid the temptation of logging on and the guilt of avoiding people because it is like a vacation. There are many types of silent retreats that include things like mediations, walks, and lectures.

2. Energize with Exercise

One of the most energetic public speakers I've ever seen is Tony Robbins. You can almost see energy radiate off him. I bet if you got close enough, you would probably hear the hum of energy.

Robbins is considered the nation's top life and business strategist. His website claims, "His work has touched the lives of top entertainers, such as Aerosmith, Green Day, Usher, and Pitbull. Billionaire business leaders seek his advice as well; casino magnate Steve Wynn and Salesforce.com founder Marc Benioff are among those who call on him for coaching."

Top business leaders listen to Robbins's advice, so when Tony talks, I listen.

Not long ago, I was fortunate to find one of Tony's podcasts on The Tim Ferriss Show. He discussed creativity and his personal routine to promote a creative state of mind.

Robbins' mantra is "change the body; change the mind." He believes if you are strong and healthy, your thoughts will be strong and healthy. The two go hand in hand. He recommends doing something extremely physical to help promote creativity, such as running, lifting weights, or swimming. Robbins says when you get the body moving, your creativity opens up.

Before he goes on stage to speak, Robbins jumps on a trampoline. This gets his heart rate up and blood flowing, which helps to clear his mind and open his creativity for whatever speech he is giving.

It is not surprising Robbin's advice for promoting creativity is activity. There is proven science that links physical activity and creative thinking. Physical activity boosts dopamine and endorphins, those neurotransmitters that produce the feel-good mojo related to creative thinking. Something as simple as taking a walk can give you that much-needed jolt of brain drugs. Another benefit of exercise is that it is a stress reliever. Exercise increases serotonin production levels, which calms the brain and leads to more creative thoughts.

Before exercise, I used to have so many thoughts spinning around my head that I often had difficulty concentrating on one thing for long. It seemed like there was constant chatter in my mind. But, when I started running long distances, I noticed my mind was silent. My thoughts seemed to float through my head one at a time. I no longer had the chaotic bombardment of thoughts, all trying to be heard at the same time. It was as if I entered a meditative state.

Think of my mind as a kindergarten class. Yes, I realize there are several jokes in that statement, but stick with me. A kindergarten class can be noisy and chaotic. The children have pent-up energy in need of an outlet. They are all trying to be heard over each other, each wanting the teacher's attention.

The teacher, being inundated from all sides, cannot hear what any individual child is saying, and therefore feels stressed and exhausted.

After recess, however, the children return to the classroom happy and relaxed. They sit quietly for story time. And they raise their hand before they speak. The teacher becomes calm and smiles.

With exercise, the brain finds its calm. It is able to sort through existing thoughts easier and more effectively create new ones. It is an effective way to cage the monkey brain.

ACTIVITY

GET PHYSICAL

Afternoons are always difficult. I would enjoy nothing more than to put my head on my desk and take a nap. That's not always an option, but brief bouts of exercise definitely is—especially during your lunch break.

Choose an activity that gets your heart rate up and that you can do during your lunch break. For example, go for a brisk walk or try hitting a few balls at the closest driving range.

Do this for a week.

At the end of the week, evaluate how you feel in the afternoon.

Are you more alert? Do you have more energy? Are you able to skip that afternoon cup of joe? Are you more productive?

Keep the activity going for a full month and evaluate how you feel in the afternoons.

Who knows, before long you'll be humming with energy like Tony Robbins.

3. Set Your Personal Space

A colleague whose job is creating innovative solutions to problems for clients shared how he generates creative ideas.

"I have found when I am doing something that does not take a lot of thought or is repetitive, like driving a familiar path or mowing the lawn, ideas seem to come easier," he said. "I also get creative ideas right before I fall asleep, or while sleeping…"

No two people are the same, so things calm and energize people in different ways. Accordingly, it is important to identify those things that prime your state of mind. If you are in the wrong state of mind, you cannot concentrate on finding creative ideas. All you see is the problem. The calmer you are, the more creative your ideas. So, how do you calm down?

First, identify the time of day when you are at your most relaxed and develop your best ideas. There is not one perfect time for everyone. Some people are relaxed in the mornings; others at night. Some people are ready for a nap by noon while others reach their stride midday as the ideas come faster than they can type.

Next, set your personal creative space. Is there a location or setting where you more easily find inspiration? Are you more creative when you are around other people, or by yourself where there is music playing? Do you require a neat and clear area, or do you like to be surrounded by items from which to pull inspiration?

Once you've answered these questions, seek out the situation that inspires creative ideas when you need them.

Famous illustrator Christopher Niemann explained in an interview the importance of understanding the environment you need to be creative.

Niemann recognizes he needs three traditional client jobs for every one creative job. He also believes it is important to push yourself out of your comfort zone to help creativity flourish. This may be having a tight deadline or working on a project that is different than your typical one.

He also recommends periodically getting out of your regular work space to boost your energy and to consider working with others whose creativity you respect. Following is a graphic that illustrates the different types of environments to help you figure out the best personal space to unleash your own creativity.

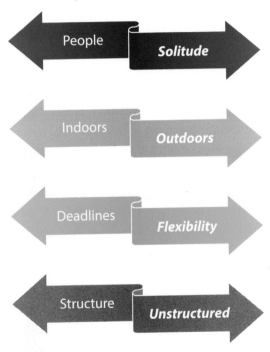

View the Quick Hits section of this book for additional ideas to relax your mind and promote creative idea generation.

4. Laughter is the Best Medicine

Comedians are among the most creative thinkers on the planet. They create humorous new ways to represent the people and situations around us. Often, their jokes are spontaneous and off-the-cuff. Watching outtakes of comedy movies with great improv artists like Jim Carrey, Jack Black, and

Robin Williams will make you laugh as much as watching the movie, but these masters of the laugh allow you to appreciate the depth and breadth of their quick thinking and world knowledge. Without a doubt, comedians possess a unique view of life—one that's both original and funny.

Not only do comedians demonstrate incredible creative thinking, but the litany of funny jokes they tell also helps promote creative thinking in others. That's right; laughing can help your creative thinking.

Recent research from the University of Western Ontario found creative thinking in others can benefit from the quick wit and humor of comedians. The study revealed that people who watched funny videos had an increased "cognitive flexibility." In layman's terms, that means they were more likely to be optimistic about various possible solutions to problems instead of being focused on just one standard solution. Scientists and psychologists refer to this phenomenon as having a "broad mental horizon."

Think back to the saga of Mr. Left Brain and Mr. Right Brain. Mr. Left Brain thought there were only a set number or solutions. It wasn't until Mr. Right Brain provided additional insight that Mr. Left Brain opened his eyes to other possibilities. Once the two started working together, the possible solutions increased. Mix in ten minutes of funny YouTube videos, and the number of possible creative solutions seems limitless.

ACTIVITIES

1 WATCH YOUTUBE

The next time you are stumped while working on a problem, set a timer for 10 minutes, log onto YouTube, and look up funny videos. Alternatively, turn on your favorite comedy TV show. You'll quickly realize the timer was important because you do not want to get sucked into YouTube and lose an hour of time.

2 FUNNIEST VIDEO

Did the short comedy break help recharge your creative thinking?

Now, try this fun twist: Start your next strategic planning or design meeting by asking a few people to share their favorite funny videos or TV clips with the group.

Vote on the funniest video.

At the end of the meeting, ask if starting the meeting with a laugh helped increase the group's open-mindedness to different ideas. I'll bet the answer is a resounding "YES!"

You Have Five Senses, Use Them All

"No idea is conceived in our mind independent of our five senses (i.e., no idea is divinely inspired)."

– *Albert Einstein*

"Nothing we use or hear or touch can be expressed in words that equal what is given by the senses."

– *Hannah Arendt, German-American philosopher and political theorist*

"Of all the senses, sight must be the most delightful."

– *Helen Keller*

"I go to nature to be soothed and healed, and to have my senses put in order."

– *John Burroughs, American naturalist and nature essayist*

"Smell is a potent wizard that transports you across thousands of miles and all the years you have lived."

– *Helen Keller*

Did you spot the consistent theme among the notable quotes above? You likely noticed every one of them had to do with one or more of the five senses. It's no coincidence that creativity relates to the senses. Now that you've learned how to calm your mind to prepare for creative thinking, it's time to explore the ways your senses can help develop creative thinking by conditioning you to pay attention to details. When you're able to do so, you'll engage your entire body and mind.

Everyone is motivated and inspired by different things. Often, the motivation is related to one of our senses. For example, as someone who enjoys the outdoors, I'm energized when a feel a cool breeze on my skin, the warm sun on my face, and the scent of spring in the air. Cooks are often motivated by complex flavors and textures. Artists find inspiration in colors and movement. What we are passionate about links back to our senses. And that holds true even if it is a lack of a sense.

I read a story about a choreographer who is inspired by silence—the lack of a sense. Her sister is deaf, so she feels passionate about creating dances that tell a story with their movement so her sister can appreciate it.

The chorographer initially develops the dance without music, only movement. Once she feels the story is appropriately conveyed though the movements of the dancers, she adds the music. As a result, the music supplements the story rather than the other way around. It is her passion and sensitivity to the lack of the sense of sound that motivates her art.

When I deliver workshops and presentations, I try to engage as many of the senses as possible for my audience. One thing I developed for this are Wake-up Bags™, beanbags made from bright colored fabric and coffee beans. They "wake up" the senses by making participants alert and engaged.

I once used them during a presentation about technical writing. Everyone loved them, and they stayed energized the entire hour session of learning how to write technical manuals! I know! Amazing, right?!

The Wake-up Bags™ seem like simple hand toys, but here is what they do:

- The bright colors attract the eyes.
- The squishiness entices touch.
- The sound of the beans intrigues the ears.
- The smell of the coffee beans stimulates the nose and triggers the brain to wake up. (Studies have shown that just the smell of coffee can help shake off sleepiness; you don't need to ingest the caffeine.)

If you'd like to make your own Wake-up Bags™, I've included directions on how to create them in the Quick Hits section of this book.

So, how do our senses activate creative thinking? Let's look at each sense to see how.

1. Let Your Nose Lead the Way

Often, when we think about learning, we only associate it with what we see or hear. However, the nose has been proven to inspire strong memories and emotional boosts. For example, the smell of rose-scented hand lotion instantly makes me think of my great-grandmother. I close my eyes, inhale deeply, and feel her large, fleshy arms wrap me in a hug. The feelings and images are very real.

The link between scent and memory is powerful. Smell can produce some of the most vivid memories we carry. Do you smile in early spring the first time you smell fresh-cut grass because you immediately think of warmer, fun-filled days?

For years, scents have been used to inspire, relax, and motivate. One need only look at the popularity of aromatherapy and the millions of dollars spent on scented candles to recognize the trend. Further, the moods and memories associated with smells can be very personal. Researchers have found that certain smells create specific reactions. In the article, "The Smell Is Right – Using Scents to Enhance Life," *Psychology Today's* Sally Augustine explains that burning frankincense can help alleviate depression while the smells of oranges can help reduce anxiety.

Augustine says you can boost creativity using the smell of cinnamon and vanilla. They will make your mind buzz with ideas. Also, the smell of lavender and frankincense have been linked to the development of serotonin in the brain, creating that calming effect, which in turn allows for more productive creative thinking.

The nose is often overlooked when seeking creative input, but using scent to stimulate the mind is an easy way to get your creative juices flowing. The next time you are stuck on a problem, feeling writer's block, or just need a motivational boost, think of a smell that gets you moving –for example, coffee. That smell may help refocus your brain. Finally, when you are learning something new, make an effort to notice the smells associated with the material—whatever is around you at that time. Then, when you need to recall the information later, your brain will have more inputs from which to pull the memory.

2. All I Need is This Fuzzy Blanket and This Paddleball Game

When you were a toddler, did you have a favorite blanket or stuffed animal? I remember my niece walking around with a blanket that had a satin edge. She loved to rub the satin on her cheek, especially when she was stressed.

Our sense of touch is one of the first ways we interact with our world. Soft and fuzzy things are soothing. Conversely, items that are sharp or hot create stress. Neither of these things go away as we grow. Do you have a favorite shirt that is well worn and soft? Is it the shirt you wear while relaxing on the couch? It should come as no surprise that something like your favorite shirt creates a relaxed state of mind, and that, subsequently, leads to increased levels of dopamine, spurring along creative thinking. Think about it. Don't you enjoy casual days at work and find it is easier to be creative than when you are wearing a stiff suit?

Another way our sense of touch helps creativity is through tactile learning. How often have you heard someone say they learn by doing, or perhaps you have noticed some people doodle while sitting in a meeting or on phone conferences. These doodles and scribbles have been proven to be beneficial in boosting creativity and helping with the retention of important information.

Lastly, playing with hand toys provides your mind with the opportunity to work through complex ideas. By doing something that is physical but not mentally taxing, it helps to cage the monkey brain. And, it allows Mr. Right Brain the opportunity to speak up and be heard. So.... get out your blankie and your paddleball game. They will boost your creativity.

3. Really See What is Around You

One of the most impactful ways we receive input is through sight. Unfortunately, people often fall into a routine and fail to notice or truly see what surrounds them. Have you ever driven home after a long, stressful day at work and not remembered the drive? That is a state most people remain in for the entire day. They go through the motions without stopping to notice the little things happening all around them. Yes, we see things, but we do not observe them.

When I run on trails in the woods, it is easy to fall into a hypnotic state. My eyes are on the shoes of the person in front of me. My ears listen to the monotonous sound of my feet striking dirt and the peaceful chirping of birds in the background. These sensory inputs are enough to make me miss miles of nature around me.

But, when I keep my mind focused, I see amazing things (and fall less). Some of the things I've seen while being observant—which I could have easily missed—include a monarch emerging from a chrysalis, a patch of bluebells, and a hidden, painted rock. These may seem like insignificant, though cool, observations, but I have recalled these specific memories in conversations with others.

For example, my sister and I saw a moth emerging from a cocoon. We got into a debate whether moths had cocoons or chrysalis. I knew I was right because I remembered seeing the monarch chrysalis on a run and researched the image when I got home. The run and the image made a connection in my mind making the information easier to recall.

Not only is being observant good for building inputs, it can also lead to a moment of inspiration. Something you see may provide the answer to a problem you left at work or a gift idea for your mom. The key is to open your eyes and see everything around you—the details of which allow you to build connections to new ideas and creative moments.

ACTIVITIES

1 A PICTURE IS WORTH A THOUSAND WORDS

Open a magazine or open an internet browser and search for a picture you like. Spend five minutes listing everything you see in the picture. How many small details can you discover?

2 WITH A PHOTOGRAPHER'S EYE

Cut out a 6" x 4" rectangle from the middle of a piece of paper. This will serve as your viewfinder.

Hold the viewfinder approximately two feet from your face and close one eye.

Look through the view finder and describe what you see.

How is this perspective different from looking at the same area without the viewfinder? How is it limiting? How does it increase what you see? Does this view invoke a different feeling or reaction than when viewing the entire area?

4. Stimulate Your Taste Buds

I love cooking shows. I'm not a great baker or chef, and I need a recipe for anything I make, but I enjoy watching the creative way chefs and bakers approach their work. For them, taste is an art, and they create unique experiences through different flavors and tastes.

Chef Gordon Ramsey on "Hell's Kitchen" cannot give a higher compliment to contestants than "You have an excellent palate." Everyone on the show aspires to hear those words. That's because if a chef has a good enough palate, he or she can recreate any dish they taste or create any flavor combination that takes patrons back to their childhood or to another country.

One of my favorite Pixar movies is "Ratatouille." In the movie, a feared food critic is brought to euphoria and near to tears, not because the dish he ate was especially tasty, but, because it took him back to his childhood when his mother made the same dish for him. The rat chef created an experience through taste.

Why do you think "comfort food" was given that name? Because it is nostalgic—what mom made provided comfort.

On the baking show "Cupcake Wars," contestants are given strange ingredients they must incorporate into a great-tasting cupcake. Only a baker who has practiced and developed his or her palate could create amazing flavor combinations such as chocolate-avocado and chocolate-mashed potato. (You must try it before you turn up your nose!)

Developing your sense of taste helps create additional connections in your memory, which in turn helps you to later make creative connections to solve issues in the future. Whether it is recalling a past memory when you savored your mom's potato soup or creating a new flavor combination, your taste buds play an important role in your creative thinking.

ACTIVITY

DEVELOP YOUR PALATE

Attend a wine or beer tasting with the goal of learning about the different flavors and notes. Make it a goal to see how many you can detect. Take some friends (and a designated driver) along with you and make it a fun experience.

What did you learn about wine or beer? What did you like about your favorite wine or beer? Did you like that same profile in others you tasted? Did any of the flavors remind you of a past experience?

5. Coffee Shops—Skip the Coffee and Go for the Noise

In the chapter about Chemical Reactions in the Brain, we explored why stimulants such as coffee, while good for focused concentration, are not conducive to creative thinking. However, this does not mean that you should avoid going to your favorite coffeehouse when you need to think creatively. Recent studies on the effects of noise on creative thinking have revealed that just as the smell of coffee can wake up your creative mind, the background noise of the coffee shop can stimulate out-of-the-box thinking.

Conducted at the University of Illinois at Urbana-Champaign, the study found that ambient noise typical of a coffee shop (around 70 decibels) enhanced the performance of participants as they brainstormed ideas for new products. This was compared to higher noise levels—85 decibels—which were deemed too distracting.

The study showed lower levels of noise, around 50 decibels, caused the participants to be too focused on the problem, and they were not able to think creatively. The lower levels of noise were perfect for focused work, which blends perfectly with the effects of caffeine on the brain as that promotes better focus rather than creativity.

So, the next time you have a problem that needs creative thinking, go to the coffeehouse to brainstorm your ideas. Once you have a few good ideas, order your favorite caffeinated drink to go and return to the quiet of your office.

With your caffeine-induced, laser-focus, you can refine your ideas and plan the implementation of your solution.

COFFEEHOUSE AND NO CAFFEINE = BETTER CREATIVE THINKING
QUIET AND CAFFEINE = FOCUSED THINKING

Another study revealed that binaural beats—the auditory illusions created when sounds of a frequency lower than 1,500 Hz are played for a listener with one sound going to each ear—also help increase creative thinking. Do a quick Google search for "binaural beats" and you'll discover they are credited with many amazing benefits—though not all scientifically proven. However, a paper from the Institute for Psychological Research and Leiden Institute for Brain and Cognition at Leiden University in the Netherlands found binaural beats presented at alpha and gamma frequency increased creative thinking and showed an increase in dopamine levels, as estimated, using spontaneous eye blink rates.

You can find playlists for binaural beats on most music websites and apps, but the key to listening is to use earbuds. Playing the binaural beats through speakers will not have the same effect. I offer some of my favorite ambient and binaural beats apps in the Quick Hits section.

TOOLBOX

APPS FOR CREATIVITY SOUNDS
There are many great apps that offer sounds to enhance creativity.
Here are two of my favorites:

Coffitivity has playlists that include ambient sounds geared toward
promoting creative thinking, such as coffee shops. The app was
developed as a result of the study by the University of Illinois at
Urbana-Champaign.

The **Spotify** app has a genre of music called Focus, which features
several playlists of soothing instrumental music and nature sounds. It
also has playlists dedicated to binaural beats for creativity.

White Noise is a free app which lets you select individual sounds, such
as rain, city traffic, and frogs, or you can create combined sounds. My
favorite sound for creative thinking is a combination of wind, chimes,
and Tibetan bowl.

PREPARE YOUR THINKING

YOU ARE NOW READY FOR THE NEXT STEP OF LEARNING THE SKILL OF CREATIVE THINKING AND IDEA GENERATION. AFTER PREPARING YOUR BODY TO BE RECEPTIVE TO CREATIVITY, YOU MUST PREPARE YOUR THINKING, AND THIS REQUIRES PRACTICE.

Creativity is a learned skill. You learn it just like you learned to read. Think back to when you first learned to read. You sounded out each letter individually. Then, as you practiced and became better, you could recognize the word without individually seeing or sounding out each letter. Through constant practice, your mind became conditioned to know the word. This holds true even if some of the letters are mixed up.

Have you ever written something and read it several times, only for someone else to point out an obvious misspelling? That's because your brain knew what the word was supposed to be and filled in the information needed without seeing each individual letter. Here's a quick exercise that illustrates this point. Read the following paragraph:

I cdn'oult blveiee taht I cluod aulaclty unesdnatnrd waht I was rdanieg the phaonmneel pweor of the hmuan mnid. Aoccdrnig to a rseearch taem at Cambrigde Uinervtisy, it deosn't mttaer in waht oredr the ltteers in a wrod are, the olny iprmoatnt tihng is taht the frist and lsat ltteer be in the rghit pclae. The rset can be a taotl mses and you can sitll raed it wouthit a porbelm. Tihs is bcuseae the huamn mnid deos not raed ervey lteter by istlef, but the wrod as wlohe. Scuh a cdonition is arppoiatrely cllaed Typoglycemia. Amzanig huh? Yaeh and you awlyas thgouht slpeling was ipmorantt.

For someone new to reading, it would have been difficult understanding the paragraph, but for someone who has practiced reading for many years, it is possible with only minimal trouble, if any. Better yet, you can apply the same concept to thinking creatively and generating ideas. You just need to practice thinking in a different way. This can be accomplished by seeing things through a new lens, finding inspiration in unexpected places, generating ideas, and making the usual connections. Here's another quick exercise that applies the same reading theory to preparing your thinking for creativity.

Look at the following list. Say the color of the word rather than the word, itself:

YELLOW·····BLUE·····ORANGE·····BLACK
RED·····GREEN·····PURPLE·····YELLOW
RED·····ORANGE·····GREEN·····BLACK
BLUE·····RED·····PURPLE·····GREEN
BLUE·····ORANGE

In the Prepare Your Thinking section of this book, you will learn to warp your mind so you can think differently. You'll be able to achieve more inputs through seeing and doing new things. You'll open your mind to new ideas, and you'll see how everything is connected. You will even notice that the topics and discussions in this section connect, overlap, and build upon other areas of this book.

Warp Your Mind

"The chief enemy of creativity is 'good sense.'"

– Pablo Picasso, artist

"Don't think. Thinking is the enemy of creativity. It's self-conscious, and anything self-conscious is lousy. You can't try to do things. You simply must do things."

– Ray Bradbury, author

"Things are only impossible until they're not."

– Jean-Luc Picard, captain, U.S.S. Enterprise
(Sure, he's a fictional character, but he's got great insight!)

"All children are artists. The problem is how to remain an artist once he grows up."

– Pablo Picasso, artist

"Creativity involve breaking out of established patterns in order to look at things in a different way."

– Edward de Bono, Maltese physician, psychologist,
philosopher, writer, inventor and consultant. He originated the term
lateral thinking and authored the book Six Thinking Hats

59

As the quotes above illustrate, in this chapter you will learn ways to alter how you think. You will learn to approach problems with a more open and creative perspective by warping your mind.

Don't be afraid.

Mind warping does not hurt, and it does not require you to hook electrodes to your head for a series of shocks or images projected into your mind.

Dr. Jack V. Matson, Emeritus Professor of Environment Engineering at Pennsylvania State University, refers to mind warping as deviating from the normal way you think. It requires you to do things differently and to take risks.

Though mind warping does not require electrodes, some of my analytical friends may still find it scary to change the way they think. So, to help ease you into this new way of thinking I've made it a three-step method:

- Be Child-like
- Practice Divergent Thinking
- Flip Your Question, Flip Your Perspective

1. Be Child-like

When I was a child, as with most children, my favorite question was "Why?"

I did not simply ask "why" once. Instead, I would continue asking "why" after every answer my parents provided.

"Why did you yell?… Well, why did the glass break?… But why did you drop it?… Why can't I come into the kitchen in my bare feet?… But why are you in the kitchen in your bare feet with broken glass on the floor?"

When I think back to all the annoying "why" questions I asked, I want to go back in time and tape my own mouth shut. I asked my parents "why" so frequently, my mom bought me a set of books called *Tell Me Why*. The set was a children's encyclopedia which answered everything from "Why is the sky blue?" to "Why do dogs spin in circles before laying down?"

There is little doubt the way children ask endless questions can become annoying, but by asking questions, children expand their creativity. As adults, if we are more childlike and ask "Why?" we open ourselves up to creatively solving problems. For example, if production is slow ask, "Why is the production line set up like this?" With that simple question, you may discover you can make a few minor changes and increase production by 1,000 units per shift.

Ty Haines, president of Manufacturer Solutions LLC and an expert in engineering, operations, and quality improvements, once told me a story about a company in desperate need of improving production time and product quality.

As Ty explained it, he visited the production floor to see the operations and noticed operators walking around the plant to retrieve tools necessary to complete repairs and changeovers on the machines.

When he asked why the necessary tools were not kept near the machines, he did not receive a satisfactory answer. The truth was, no one had thought to store the tools in a central location. No one questioned why the tools were not stored in one place close to the operators who needed them.

Did this one change resolve all the issues the plant faced?

No, but it was a quick and simple fix with significant impact, and it was the result of asking one simple question: Why?

Being childlike is not only about asking why. It also means letting go of preconceived notions. In his book *How to Get Ideas*, Jack Foster wrote, "The adult thinks too much and has too much scar tissue and is manacled by too much knowledge and by too many boundaries and rules and assumption and preconceptions."

Foster continued that the child is "innocent and free and does not know what he cannot or should not do. He sees the world as it is and not the way adults have been taught it is."

As adults, we tend to assume boundaries and constraints when none exist. The perfect example is the nine dots puzzle.

ACTIVITIES

NINE DOT PUZZLE
Connect all nine dots using only four lines. Do not lift your pencil or retrace over any lines.

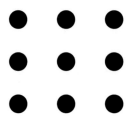

(Answer: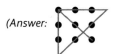

This is an old puzzle. You may have known the solution already, but the lesson is appropriate: Most adults assume that when drawing the four lines you must remain within the 3 X 3 grid. This is a preconceived constraint which makes the puzzle impossible to complete. Only people who break out of this assumption can solve the puzzle.

Despite this, some limits are helpful for the creative process, including deadlines and budgets. These provide a framework in which you can work. However, it is important to be careful in assuming constraints which do not exist.

The last lesson we can learn by being childlike is to not fear appearing silly.

One of my favorite "Friends" episodes is when Phoebe ran through Central Park looking like a cross between Kermit the Frog and the Six Million Dollar Man because of how she screams and waves her arms.

Rachel is mortified Phoebe acts like this in public.

But Phoebe replies, "I can see why running with me would be embarrassing to you. You're uptight... I'm more free. I run like I did when I was a kid because that's the only way it's fun."

Phoebe does not care how her running looks. She is not afraid to look silly. Neither are children. Just watch them at play.

How does this apply to creativity?

Simple. The more creative your solutions, the more people will question them, and the more your creative ideas will be ridiculed and laughed at.

Have you ever heard of the Fosbury Flop? Sounds funny, right? Many people laughed at Dick Fosbury because of it... until he won the gold medal in the 1968 Summer Olympics using the Fosbury Flop during the high jump event.

Until Fosbury, most high jumpers cleared the bar using a scissor or straddle jump or a roll. Fosbury, by contrast, ran up to the bar, curved around at the last second and flopped his body over.

In action, the jump is as funny looking as Pheobe's running, but it is highly effective. Fosbury did not allow the laughter and ridicule to stop him from performing what he knew to be a superior high jump method. After winning the gold medal, the Fosbury Flop became the predominate method used.

So, what happens when someone creates a new and innovative product? Often, it is viewed as funny or useless. People label it foolish or even impractical. Do you think we would have personal computers, airplanes, or indoor plumbing if people feared looking silly?

Be creative.

Be bold.

Experience creative anxiety and ridicule of others.

Most of all, be fearless.

TOOLBOX

BREAK OUT OF ASSUMPTIONS WORKSHEET
To help you avoid making unnecessary assumptions and constraints about a problem, ask the following questions:

1. What assumptions/constraints am I making?
2. What assumptions/constraints am I not making?
3. What assumptions/constraints give me what I see?

Then ask:
1. How might I solve it now?
2. What assumptions/constraints am I not aware I am making?
3. What solution(s) would provide other options?

ACTIVITY

EXPLAIN IT TO A SIX-YEAR-OLD
Think of a problem of any complexity that you have at home or at work. Pretend you must explain the problem to a six-year-old.

What would you say?

How might the six-year-old tell you to solve the problem?

2. Practice Divergent Thinking

Growing up, we are drilled to think analytically, sequentially, and in words. Timed math tests and memorization are good examples of this in action. This type of thinking is great for learning a list of facts, such as the order of the Presidents, historical timelines, and company products. However, developing solutions to complex problems requires different methods of thinking: visual, lateral, and ambidextrous.

The way you think affects **what** you think and the types of thoughts you get.

When you think in pictures, you can manipulate the data and visualize different outcomes before moving forward with a solution. Some people are naturally visual thinkers. If you are not a visual thinker, this takes practice.

You can practice visual thinking by keeping a piece of paper nearby. Sketch the problem; then draw what various solutions would look like. This is visual thinking.

While thinking in pictures is self-explanatory, understanding lateral and ambidexterity thinking is a little different. In its simplest form, lateral thinking is the opposite of linear thinking; and ambidexterity thinking is engaging the non-dominate side of your mind.

Lateral thinking was popularized by Edward de Bano, a physician, psychologist, and author. He encouraged people to make jumps and take side roads in their thinking instead of following a logical, sequential, "if-then" path. Think of it as the Family Circus comic, which showed the little boy's route from the park to home.

In Family Circus, the dotted line the boy traveled did not remain on the sidewalk, even though he only needed to travel two blocks to get to his house. Rather, the dotted line cut through yards, over fences, around trees and through leaf piles. It crossed the street to hop through mud puddles before finally turning into the house. At the end, the boy was wet, dirty, and smiling because of the adventure of his journey. When thinking lateral, allow your mind to cross the street to splash in the mud puddles and see what solutions turn up.

To practice lateral thinking, try mind mapping problems. Mind mapping is a common practice in problem solving, but you must do it properly to promote lateral thinking. This means that to truly get your mind jumping and taking side-roads, you must use words, pictures, colors, symbols, and anything else that comes to mind. Most importantly, do not censor your thoughts.

If you have never mind mapped, it is easy to learn.

Start with the main topic or problem in the center of a white space. I prefer using a large whiteboard. As you think of possible solutions, write or draw them around the center issue. Use a line to connect it to the center, and again, don't censor your ideas—no matter how crazy they may seem. Let your mind go where it wants. You may think of new solutions, or a solution you devise may take your mind down a different path.

Capture all the thoughts and then use lines to connect them to the origin of the fork-in-the-road. See the following illustration for an example.

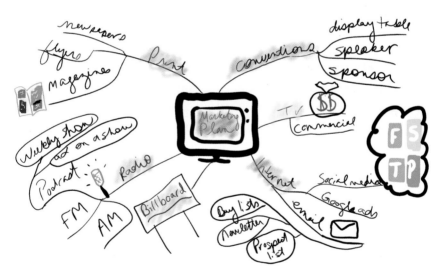

The last method of divergent thinking is ambidexterity thinking.

At some point, most people have heard the theory about how the right side of the brain controls the muscles on the left side of the body and the left side of the brain controls the muscles on the right side of the body.

So, to get your entire brain working on a problem, you need ambidexterity thinking.

In the book, *How to Think Like Leonardo da Vinci*, Professor Raymond Dart says, "Balance the body, balance the brain. The future lies with the ambidextrous human!"

Renaissance artists were known to paint both right- and left-handed. Leonardo da Vinci regularly practiced mirror writing (writing backwards on a page from the right to the left). People who apply the entire brain to working on a problem are the innovators.

Learning ambidexterity is easier than most people think. Talk to a baby-boomer and you will hear stories of left-handed children being forced to use their right hand. Their handwriting was messy at first, but they adapted.

When I was a toddler, I was left handed... until I broke my left arm when I was three. I wore a plaster cast over my entire arm and hand. It only left the first two joints of my fingers visible. Using my left hand to write or draw was impossible. Over those six weeks, I started using my right hand to color, eat, and brush my teeth. When the cast was removed, I continued to use my right hand. However, there are certain tasks that, to this day, I prefer to do left-handed, such as shoot pool and sink a putt in golf.

When I was in my twenties, I sliced my thumb and first finger on my right hand, which made writing difficult. I attempted to write with my left hand and was surprised at how quickly I adapted to it. With practice you can teach your whole mind to activate on command.

For a fun way to practice ambidexterity thinking, try mirror writing like Leonardo da Vinci with your non-dominate hand.

THINKING INSIDE THE BOX

You recall the nine-dot puzzle. The following is a more creative approach to that puzzle. The original puzzle only allows for one solution. This puzzle allows for many solutions. The dots are simply guidelines. Your lines do not need to follow or even touch the dots. You don't even need to use straight lines.

Your objective is to discover as many ways as possible to divide a square into four equal parts. The first square is completed for you as an example (and because it is much too easy). Use your new, creative methods of thinking to divide the remaining squares.

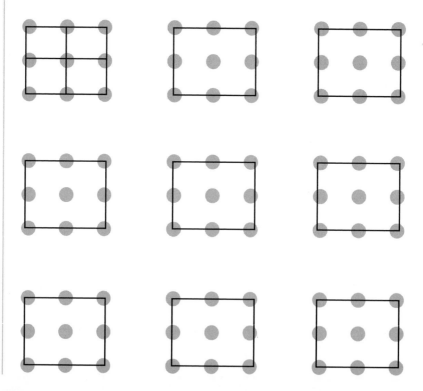

3. Flip Your Questions, Flip Your Perspective

The last phase in warping your mind is to flip your perspective. You can do this by asking yourself an entirely new set of questions. Different questions allow you to see unique ways in which items are related and to include novelty with necessity.

My friend Ty Haines offered a great example of changing your perspective: He was tasked with improving the suction of a vacuum without increasing the production costs.

The first impulse is to start thinking of ways to increase the motor power and increase the airflow CMF (cubic feet per minute). Once you have a few ideas, you calculate costs and discard any that are more expensive than the original production costs. With this method of thinking, you are left with very little, if any, ways to improve the vacuum cleaner.

An alternative method is to change the question.

Instead of the first question being the obvious "How can we improve the motor power and airflow CFM?" ask "What items on the vacuum can easily be made less expensive without affecting the functionality?"

This question provides an increased budget to consider more methods for improving the vacuum suction. When Ty asked this question, he realized that the fancy chrome molding on the cleaner was purely aesthetic, and a plastic, less expensive molding could be used instead.

By changing the question and looking at the problem from a different perspective, Ty's company could provide the customers with what they really wanted from a vacuum cleaner: better suction.

Let's look at another example of flipping your perspective by flipping your questions.

At BrainSpark, the company where I work, whenever there is a new idea we want to try or an issue to solve, instead of stating it as a sentence and then reviewing the obstacles in our way, we flip it and ask the question "How can we..." It is amazing how many of the barriers disappear once we change our perspective and questions.

This method also eliminates a lot of the defensiveness and ego people have when it is their area having the issue or when their idea is not selected to move forward. It also provides a forum for creative solutions.

Of course, not all solutions are appropriate, but, by thinking differently, you have many more options from which to choose.

We were inspired to adapt this method by the book *Change Your Questions, Change Your Life*, by Marilee Adams. Here are just a few examples of how this method works:

Billable hours are down.	How can we increase billable hours?
• Suspend vacations. • Sell more.	• Consultants can help clients gather source materials and review documents to increase hours and speed up project timelines. • Approve overtime for hourly employees. • Negotiate rates with prospects to close contracts that have not closed. • Contact existing clients to see if they need help in other areas.
Employees want software training, but it's not in the budget.	How can we provide the employees with software training?
• Tell them they must learn it on their own. • Consider it for next year's budget.	• Ask if one of the existing employees would teach the others about the software. • Research what free training is available online. • Conduct a one-hour webinar during lunch time once a week.

As you see from the examples, flipping your perspective provides new associations that under normal practice you would not make. It is unexpected logic, creative thinking, and may lead to innovative solutions.

Google originally wanted to be the best search engine. It succeeded, but the company executives knew to continue being successful they needed to find additional ways to grow the company.

Google's mission is "to organize the world's information and make it universally accessible and useful." That mission seems to pigeon-hole the company to its existing search engine, but when viewed from a different perspective, the executives realized there was more to the world's information than simply websites.

As a result, Google products now include Google Earth, Google Book Search, Google Alert, Google Maps, and many more.

TOOLBOX

MIND WARPING QUESTIONS

Following is a list of simple questions that can have big results and can help you flip your perspective. It is not an all-inclusive list, but it will get you started on developing your own flipped questions.

- Why not?
- How can I...?
- What changes could be made?
- What does the customer really want and what do they need?
- What issues would be solved by doing that?
- How can I improve this?
- How can I make this less expensive?
- What are other people doing?
- What can I learn from past failures?
- How can I make this fun?

ACTIVITIES

1 UNEXPECTED LOGIC

1. Look at the following list of words and sort them into categories. You determine what and how many categories.

digit	subtraction	number
division	rectangle	addition
equality	pi	millimeter
circle	form	point
pyramid	surface	area
twenty-three	diagonal	derivative
theorem	curve	decimal
fraction	side	percentage
volume	diameter	zero
straight line	limit	edge
infinite	angle	
equation	denominator	
perimeter	cone	

2. Next, review your categories. Most people, when sorting the list create logical categories such as Numbers, Shapes, and Formulas. If that's what you did then look at the list again and think of different ways that you can sort the words. Maybe you could categorize them by opposites or by the number of letters of the word.

2 DESIGN A BATHROOM

This activity practices looking at an issue through someone else's perspective.

Scenario: You won a contest and have been given the opportunity to redesign your bathroom for free. The company sponsoring the contest is willing to have anything manufactured for your dream bathroom as publicity to support their tagline "If you dream it, we can build it."

You are extremely excited about this opportunity because you are 6′ 9″ tall and this is your chance to have a bathroom built for your height. The existing bathroom space you have to work with is 10′ x 10′.

1. In five minutes, write everything you want in your dream bathroom. Continue writing for the entire five minutes without stopping. Don't worry about being absurd or unrealistic. Consider the difficulties a person of that height would have. Don't forget to include plenty of luxury items in the bathroom!

2. After the five minutes, review your list of ideas. You will probably notice the first items on your list are obvious solutions to your height problem. However, as the time ticked, your ideas may have slowed... but they also started becoming more creative. These ideas may be unusual, unrealistic, or fantastic, but you can ask how they might be created later. For now, you've begun the creativity process, and that leads to opportunities you otherwise might not have imagined.

③ A SUPERHERO IN SUBURBIA
This activity will help put everything you learned about flipping your perspective into use. You are going to write a story. While writing the story, practice asking questions, making new associations, and looking at the situation from a different perspective.

1. You are a Superhero living in suburbia. You choose your superpower.

2. Write what a typical, average day looks like for a superhero living in suburbia: lawns need to be mowed, floors need to be swept, kids need to be fed.

3. Your story must obey the laws of society and physics, except for your superpower.

4. You must keep your identity secret.

Another way to flip your perspective is to look at the situation from someone or something else's viewpoint. This not only leads to additional ideas, but can also add novelty. Solutions, by their very nature, do not always have to have a practical solution. Sometimes, the solution is simply to add fun or luxury. When you ask, "What does the customer want and what does the customer need?" you sometimes learn the customer wants things which often have nothing to do with what they need. Sometimes, the customer is willing to pay more money for a vacuum cleaner with greater suction and shiny chrome. By looking at the issue from the customer's perspective, you open additional potential solutions.

If you have a complex issue to explain, and you are not sure how to get your message across, pretend you are a 10-year-old explaining the issue.

As adults, we tend to make issues more complicated than they need to be. When you are 10, you simplify details and refrain from using jargon.

Or, consider looking at the situation from the perspective of an inanimate object?

This is an excellent method to flip your perspective and get creative ideas. If you need to figure out a new design for bookbags for the new school year, pretend you are a bookbag. What problems do you have? What things do you hate? What are you good at?

My first thought was that my straps are too long and the kindergartener that purchased me drags me through the dirt and down the sidewalk. Within a week, I will have holes and be filthy.

When you warp your thinking, it is important initially that you do not censor yourself by thinking "That is dumb" or "That is unrealistic." Remember, the purpose is to increase your creativity and identify as many ideas as possible. During this stage of the process, anything is acceptable. Narrowing down the ideas comes later, when you ask "How can we?" to the ones that interest you.

Get More Inputs

"Creativity is about making a lot of quick connections—about things you know, the things you've seen. The more you've done, the easier it is to make that jump."

– Jerry Della Femina

"If you want to be creative go where your questions lead you. Do things. Have a wide variety of experiences."

– Louis L'Amour

"Around here, however, we don't look backwards for very long. We keep moving forward, opening up new doors and doing new things, because we're curious... and curiosity keeps leading us down new paths."

– Walt Disney

"Everything is theoretically impossible, until it is done."

– Robert A. Heinlein

As the quotes above illustrate, creative people always seem to be doing or working on something interesting and outside the realm of the every day. I've been accused of having too many hobbies because at any given time I'll be working on a quilt, training for an ultramarathon, planning a backpacking trip, reading about the birth of computers, and taking a hip-hop dancing class (much to my daughter's embarrassment).

When discussing creative people, a few common descriptions come to mind: they're curious, and they're courageous. They ask questions and look things up. They are interested in knowing a little about a lot of topics.

However, I would push back a bit on this as an oversimplification. While people say these things are the nature of a creative person, I believe that instead, it is these activities which make a person creative. They provide numerous inputs for the brain. Accordingly, when the time comes, the brain is prompted to generate creative solutions to the problems being faced.

When our creative mind is working, it is actively looking for the right inputs necessary to apply to whatever problem is being considered. Think about a time you faced a problem. Let's say it was something relatively mundane: trying to figure out what to buy your mother for her birthday.

Imagine yourself trying to decide what would make the perfect gift. Where do your eyes go? Do you look around hoping something will spark an idea? Do you look off into space and mentally catalogue the gifts your mom liked and disliked in the past? Are you thinking about your mother's hobbies and interests?

When you search your surroundings and your memory, your creative brain is seeking inputs. It looks for inspiration in your surroundings, memories, and experiences. What follows is an exploration of how curiosity and getting additional inputs help generate more creative ideas, as well as what you can do to get a wider variety of inputs.

1. How Multiple Inputs Expand Creativity

Early in the book I explained the parts of the brain at work during creative thinking and the chemical reactions that occur. But there are also important things happening inside the brain when you use multiple inputs for information.

Recall (or flip back to The Science Behind Creativity section) that when the analytical side of your brain rests, the creative—or right-side—of your brain takes over. This is when the moments of insight occur.

One method to get your left brain to quiet enough for the right brain to provide answers is to use cognitive diversity. Clive Thompson, author of the book *Smarter Than You Think*, explains cognitive diversity as the type of thinking that occurs when you do something differently than how you would normally do it. He explains that using cognitive diversity stimulates areas of your brain which have been less than active, while at the same time providing the more active parts a mental break. This creates those moments of inspiration.

This is why brainstorming, drawing, and talking to colleagues can often help your brain make connections it did not see before. It also sparks your ability to develop a creative solution to a problem. By seeking additional inputs of information, you create cognitive diversity, which stimulates your brain and sparks creativity.

In the same chapter, I explored the correlation among dopamine and creativity. Dopamine activates the parts of the brain related to creativity, memory, and pleasure. According to research led by Charan Ranganath at the University of California, dopamine is released into the brain when we become overly curious. Since curiosity activates our memory and pleasure, the effects of learning something you are curious about makes you feel good, and you are more likely to remember it. The increase in memory and mental stimulation in turn creates various inputs of information which can be used to draw upon, thus strengthening creativity.

Now, let's look at ways to get more inputs.

2. Be Curious. Ask Questions

Creative people aren't curious. Curiosity creates creative people. So, don't be afraid to ask questions. Working in the consulting business, clients expect me to be an expert. Early in my career, I translated this to mean I should act like I knew exactly what people were talking about… even if I was clueless. This led to misunderstandings, projects taking longer than they should, and some mistakes.

When I finally understood that it is acceptable and better to ask questions rather than project that I knew all the answers, my work improved and I was much more of the expert clients expected.

Questions not only help the quality of your work by getting you answers, they also help develop your creativity. Do not be afraid to ask how something works, or why a specific process is used. Learn to ask different types of questions, such as "what if…" Sometimes, in the answer you will find there is a better solution. Or, that answer will lead you down a divergent path of thinking, where you discover innovative ideas.

Only by asking a question to which your brain does not automatically have the answer are you are forced to think of the subject from a new perspective, and this is where creativity begins to flourish.

Here's an example: The CEO of a national tire retailer asked his executive board to find a way to cut the costs of used tire disposal, which was running in the millions of dollars.

Members of the CEO's executive team took the problem to key people in their departments and asked for their thoughts and ideas.

Not surprisingly, it was an accountant who discovered a viable solution. What was surprising, however, was the creativity he used to land on the solution.

Instead of answering the question "How can we save money on used tire disposal?", the accountant posed a new question. He asked, "How can we make money while disposing of the used tires?"

Nobody had thought to consider the issue from this perspective. Everyone was focused on saving money and cutting costs. But he saw things differently. And by approaching the issue in this manner—and conducting some research— he discovered there was a small company that accepted used tires for free. The company shred the tires and sold the shredded tire pieces as an alternative to the traditional mulch used for covering the ground at playgrounds.

The accountant provided the information to the executive team and posited a bold solution to their problem: acquire the tire shredding company.

By purchasing the small tire shredding company, the national tire sellers quickly went from losing money to making a profit from used tire disposal. But this only happened because one person within the organization changed the approach to asking questions about how to solve the problem. There are dozens of similar stories of organizations that approached problem solving through creativity.

Another thing I learned in my years as a consultant is how much clients that are considered the subject matter experts LOVE to talk about their process, project, device, or product. They are passionate people! I don't bring this up as a negative, but rather a positive. The people who are closest to the subject AND enjoy telling a willing and active listener the details of how something was developed, the issues of getting executive buy-in, and all the minutiae of their world, can help spark the creative process.

Encourage them to talk, so you get as much information as you can.

Ask the go-to interview questions of who, what, why, where, when, and how. Most of the information you cull may not be needed immediately, but the more information you collect, the more diverse your toolbox will be when you need to draw from it later.

Some people may call this having a head full of useless information, but I call it being prepared. As the cartoon character G.I Joe said, "Knowing is half the battle." Be curious and ask questions and you'll find you have a treasure trove of creative ammunition to fire at whatever problems you encounter.

ACTIVITY

THERE ARE NO BAD QUESTIONS

This exercise acclimates you to asking questions. As we grow and become adults, we ask less questions. Adults feel embarrassed and concerned they will be ridiculed for not knowing the answer. Kids don't face this— they keep asking question after question.

This activity also helps you to approach life from a new perspective so that you can get more inputs.

1. For the next 5 minutes, write as many odd or silly questions as you can think of. For example, what would my dog say to me if he could talk? What would the world be like if our main building material was marshmallows? If I had wings where would I go?
2. Then, for fun, choose one of the questions and create an answer.

TOOLBOX

CURIOSITY QUIZ

Fortune 500 companies want to hire highly creative people to help develop innovative solutions to the problems they face. Some companies have started using curiosity quizzes as part of their process to weed out less creative people. They've recognized that curiosity fuels creativity, which in turn ignites innovation.

Here is a "yes" or "no" quiz adapted from the Harvard Business Review, designed to help you determine how curious you are and identify areas for improvement. See how strong your curiosity is, and whether you're taking the time to nurture it.

1. For each statement, check the Yes box if it is true for you, or check No if it is not true for you.
2. Select one of the statements you marked as No and work on developing that skill.

	Yes	No
I take adequate time for contemplation and reflection.		
I am always learning something new.		
When I am faced with an important decision, I actively seek out different perspectives.		
I am voracious reader.		
I learn from little children.		
I'll try anything once to see what it's like.		
I am skilled at identifying and solving problems.		
My friends would describe me as open-minded and curious.		
I ask questions.		
I enjoy talking to strangers.		

	Yes	No
When I hear or read a new word or phrase I look it up and make a note of it.		
I know a lot about other cultures and am always learning more.		
I know or am learning a language other than my native one.		
I solicit feedback from my friends, relations, and colleagues.		
I love learning.		
I ask how things work.		
I love the excitement of the unknown.		
I like meeting new people.		

3. Be Courageous. Try Something New

The best and easiest way to get more inputs is trying new things. New experiences awaken and strengthen creativity by kicking in dopamine and building memories for your creative mind to draw upon.

Many people think inspiration only comes from activities such as sitting in a park surrounded by nature, but the truth is that inspiration is your mind making neuronal connections. Maybe it is the quiet park which allows your left brain to quiet and your right brain to be heard, but first it needs inputs to make connections.

Napoleon Hill, a self-help author, wrote in his book *Think and Grow Rich* the following: "Your subconscious mind recognizes and acts upon only thoughts which have been well-mixed with emotion or feeling… You will get no appreciable results until you learn to reach your subconscious mind with thoughts or spoken words which have been well emotionalized with belief."

Hill's assertion is that you must feed your subconscious mind with a variety of inputs—emotions and feelings. These come from experiences: things you do, shows you watch, books you read, conversations you have. To get these inputs, you need to leave your safe confines and experience what is out there. Getting out of your comfort-zone and being courageous enough to try something completely different. These may include learning about new subjects, participating in activities, meeting and speaking with people, seeing new sights, and paying attention to smells. The more variety you add to your experiences, the more creative the neuronal connections your brain creates.

Bill Evans is an amazing jazz pianist. Jazz is known for improvisation. Even though improv is making something up on the spot (a courageous act in itself), its roots come from experience. Without experience, a jazz musician would not have a song and a comedian would not have an act. Evans said this about being courageous: "You can be overly cautious to a point where you never discover anything."

He has a point.

ACTIVITY

30 DAY CHALLENGE
For the next 30 days, try to do something new every day. It can be big or small, but it must be something you have never done before.

Here are a few examples:
- Learn to play a tune on a harmonica
- Try a new restaurant
- Read an article on the Internet about a topic you know nothing about
- Have a conversation with a stranger

If you have trouble thinking of new things to try, the following **TOOLBOX: New Things to Try** may help spark a few ideas.

TOOLBOX

NEW THINGS TO TRY

1. Read a book or article about a subject in which you have an interest, but you do not know much about. Examples:
   a. History of World War II
   b. The invention of indoor plumbing
   c. Computer programming
   d. Moose
   e. Walt Disney
   f. Indigenous people of the South Pacific
   g. What was the wild west really like?
   h. Women's fashion through the ages
   i. The evolution of rock and roll
   j. Animals that live in caves

2. Listen to a new genre of music. Examples:
   a. New age / meditation
   b. Electronic
   c. Hip-hop
   d. Latino
   e. Country
   f. Classical
   g. Jazz
   h. Funk
   i. Oldies
   j. Instrumental

3. Take a class to learn a new skill. Examples:
   a. Playing a harmonica
   b. Speaking Mandarin
   c. Sushi making
   d. Ballroom dance
   e. Knot tying
   f. Bird identification
   g. Retirement planning
   h. Nutrition
   i. Painting
   j. Edible plant identification

4. Take up a new hobby. Examples:
   a. Quilting
   b. Backpacking
   c. Gardening
   d. Running
   e. Stamp collecting
   f. Antiquing
   g. Stand-up Paddle Boarding
   h. Roasting coffee
   i. Woodworking
   j. Glassblowing

Become Idea Prone

"Whatever the mind can conceive and believe, the mind can achieve."

– Napoleon Hill

"There's always another idea, always another solution. Accept it."

– Jack Foster

"The way to get good ideas is to get lots of ideas and throw the bad ones away."

– Linus Pauling

"You can't use up creativity. The more you use the more you have."

– Maya Angelou

"Capital isn't so important in business. Experience isn't so important. You can get both these things. What is important is ideas. If you have ideas, you have the main asset you need, and there isn't any limit to what you can do with your business and your life."

– Harvey Firestone

You cannot expect inspiration to strike on your timetable. Just as with all the methods so far mentioned on conditioning your mind to be creative, you need to practice becoming idea prone. The more accustomed you are to forming ideas, the more ideas you will have.

Many of the worlds' best thinkers and intelligent problem-solvers do something every day to practice being idea prone. If you practice generating ideas, you are more likely to generate quality ideas when you need them.

Why do you want to get more ideas?

The more accustomed you are to generating ideas, the more moments of inspiration you will have. Ideas lead to solutions. Ideas lead to innovative products and processes. Ideas create progress.

In this section, we will explore how you can practice generating more ideas, which in turn lead to more high quality, innovative solutions.

1. Don't Overthink

Often when faced with solving a problem, we become stuck trying to find a solution. You've heard the expression writer's block? Well, it occurs with everyone, not just writers. The best definition would be when we try to force an idea or a moment of inspiration to happen... but nothing comes to mind.

When this happens, there are some simple ways to reset the situation. First, step back and relax your mind. Next, stop overthinking the problem and then write down as many solutions as you can—whether plausible or not.

This process is effective working by yourself or in a group. Either way, during the "idea dump" phase, do not discount any idea. The initial goal should be to achieve quantity over quality. We'll discuss how to narrow down the list and fine-tune the best ideas, later.

Bob McKim, once a lead at the Stanford Design Program, created an activity to get students out of the initial hesitation they experience around drawing. He identified this initial hesitation as overthinking.

What if I'm not good enough?

What style should I use?

What if the person I draw is offended by my depiction?

In response, McKim instructed his students to draw the person sitting next to them... but with a 30-second time limit. Adding the time limit removed the chance that the students would spend too much thinking about the drawing, and it eliminated any opportunity for them to critique their own work.

The results?

McKim found that by adding the time limit his students produced more creative work.

The following exercise is similar to McKim's activity. It is based on the 30 Circles exercise used by IDEO, a design company. This exercise should help you stop overthinking or self-critiquing and jump directly into idea generation.

20 CIRCLES

For this activity, you need to photocopy the pages of circles in the Quick Hits section of this book or create your own on a piece of paper. If you opt to create your own, draw 20 circles approximately 1 ½" in diameter on the paper. Use additional pieces of paper if necessary to reach 20 circles.

You also need a writing instrument—a pencil, pen, marker, etc.— and a timer.

1. Set the timer for three minutes.
2. Within those three minutes, draw inside each circle to turn it into something different. For example, turn the first circle into a smiley face and the second into a baseball. Do this with as many of the circles as you can—creating different objects for each circle. Do not duplicate.
3. At the end of three minutes, count how many circles you completed. Did you transform all 20 circles? If not, that is OK. It takes practice to generate ideas.
4. Take a break and try again.

How did you do the second time? Did you increase the number of circles you transformed?

2. Transitioning Between Left and Right

Remember that rush of ideas that comes when you initially apply yourself to problem-solving efforts? When it happens, you may have so many ideas at one time that you have difficulty capturing them fast enough. And, recall that after the initial rush of ideas, you probably started to slow down. Think about the slow down during the 20 Circles Activity: Did you find yourself looking around the room for an idea? Now consider this: If you had more time, would you experience a second rush of ideas? Yes, you probably would. This is a common cycle in idea generation.

In the Science Behind Creativity section, I introduced Mr. Left Brain and Mr. Right Brain and demonstrated each side's role in creativity. The idea generation exercises are good examples of these two gentlemen at work.

The initial rush of ideas is Mr. Left Brain spouting off all the information he's gathered over his many years of experience. The pause is the transition to Mr. Right Brain. He is new, and his ideas are untested and different. It takes him a few minutes before he gains confidence and really starts pushing out the ideas. Once he does, the ideas begin to flow again.

But there is a sweet-spot in this process, and it's one that all idea-generators want to achieve. It occurs when Mr. Left Brain sets aside his ego and listens to Mr. Right Brain. They begin to work together to generate a few solid ideas.

While these ideas may not be as plentiful as a traditional brain-storming session, they have the advantage of input from both sides of your brain: the inspiration of Mr. Right Brain and the experience of Mr. Left Brain. It looks a little like this:

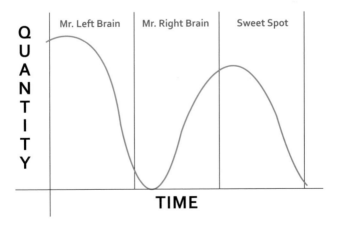

BRAINSPARKING

Most people are familiar with the process of brainstorming to generate ideas. It works like this: Either alone or with a group you write as many ideas as possible without thinking about the details. Sometimes, people use sticky notes to write ideas. Other times, they create a mindmap. And then there's the traditional way of writing down all the ideas in list form—on a whiteboard, sheet of paper, laptop, tablet, or other means of capturing them.

Recent articles have attempted to discredit the effectiveness of brainstorming, but with a few guidelines, this can be a very valuable process for generating a lot of solutions.

It's brainstorming smarter.

It's BrainSparking!

Here are the guidelines:

1. **Don't solve.** During this phase the goal is not to solve the problem but to generate as many ideas as possible. Think quantity over quality, which may be difficult for a perfectionist, but you must learn to let it go.
2. **Avoid judging.** At this point, every idea is a good idea—whether you are working in a group of by yourself.
3. **Capture every idea.** If you are brainstorming by yourself, capture every idea generated. If you are working in a group, designate one person to write them on a whiteboard, flipchart, or sticky notes; or have everyone write their own idea but state out loud their idea once it has been captured.
4. **Number the ideas.** While you capture the ideas, number them. For motivation, you can set a prize if a specific number of ideas is generated.

5. **Set a time limit.** This keeps a focus on the generation of ideas and helps reign in judgement and logistic-thinking. Plus, it keeps you from overthinking.

6. **Avoid discussion.** The clock is ticking. Now is not the time to discuss the relevance or the application of the idea. Just keep generating more ideas.

7. **Be specific.** You want to provide enough detail so that when the ideas are reviewed later, anyone can look at it and understand what the captured idea means. There is nothing worse than having a great idea and then not be able to recall it later.

8. **Build on ideas.** Look at the captured ideas for inspiration for other ideas. How can you alter the idea a little to create a new idea? Is there a theme emerging that you can use to develop more ideas?

9. **Participate.** If you are working in a group, do not let everyone else do all the work. Do not be shy. Remember, no idea is a bad idea. Throw yours out there. It may end up being the perfect solution or it may inspire a new line of thinking that leads to the eventual solution.

ACTIVITY

IDEA JOURNAL
How do you get to Carnegie Hall?

Practice.
I know I mentioned that joke earlier but it is true and an important lesson. Let me say it again: PRACTICE!

Generating ideas happens the same way. It takes practice. One way to practice generating ideas is to start keeping an idea journal.

89

1. First, get a notebook and write "Idea Journal" on the cover.
2. Next, write today's date on the first page at the top.
3. Now, write three ideas.
   Your ideas can be anything—an idea for a story, a solution to a problem at work, or even a device which would automatically water your flower pots. Do not concern yourself with whether you know how to implement your idea or if it seems silly. Right now, the purpose of this exercise is to condition your thinking to be idea prone. The quality of ideas comes later with practice.
4. Over the next seven days, write the current date on a new page in the notebook and increase the number of ideas by one for each subsequent day. On Day Eight, you will generate a total of 10 new ideas.
5. At the end of the first week, you should have generated 52 ideas. Review your ideas and highlight the ones you would like to develop further or research more.
6. Continue to generate 10 new ideas each day for the next three weeks. Write them in your notebook. At the end of each week, review your ideas and highlight the ones you think are good.
7. Then, at the end of the month, review all your ideas.

Did you notice an increase in quality? Are you generating your daily 10 ideas any quicker? Are there any patterns or themes to the ideas? Are you likely to act on any of them?

8. Now, set a new goal for your idea journal. You decide on the new goal. This may be an attempt to increase the number of ideas by five each week for the next month, maintain the idea journal for the rest of the year, or even use the idea journal at work to document problems and ideas for solutions.

9. Keep generating ideas in the journal and soon you will discover that you have greatly improved your idea generation abilities.

3. Improve Upon Existing Ideas

By now, you've probably recognized the fodder for ideas is everywhere. However, there are people who believe all the best ideas have already been discovered. It is my belief, however, that those people are simply not aware that new ideas exist—let's call it blissful ignorance.

Have you noticed that once you are aware a solution to a problem exists, you get a dozen ideas about other solutions? However, when you are told a solution is impossible you cannot think of a single idea? It's a pretty simple concept: People that get ideas know they exist; those who don't get ideas, don't know they exist.

The reality is that for every problem, there are hundreds of solutions, answers, ideas, and additional problems with additional solutions, answers, and ideas. One of my favorite quotes that illustrates this theory is by the 20th century New York reporter Lincoln Steffens:

> "Nothing is done. Everything in the world remains to be done or done over. The greatest picture is not yet painted, the greatest play isn't written, the greatest poem is unsung. There isn't in all the world a perfect railroad, nor a good government, nor a sound law. Physics, mathematics, and especially the most advanced and exact of sciences, are being fundamentally revised. Chemistry is just becoming a science; psychology, economics, and sociology are awaiting a Darwin, whose work in turn is awaiting an Einstein. If the rah-rah boys in our colleges could be told this, they might not all be specialists in football, parties, and unearned degrees. They are not told it, however; they are told to learn what is known. This is nothing."

This is beautifully stated.

Instead of teaching our children to regurgitate known facts and ideas, we should teach them to use those facts and ideas to spark new, creative ideas that lead to innovative products and processes to solve modern problems. In fact, we need to teach our children how to solve the problems we haven't yet imagined.

Consider the advancement of the mobile phone.

In the early 1990s, only the uber-rich and important people had a car phone. It was connected by a cord to the car, itself, and was slightly smaller than the size of a shoe box. Over the last 30 years, we have witnessed major changes and improvements in the mobile phone industry to the point that your phone is also a camera, computer, radio, and gaming device in one small package.

But the modern mobile phone is not the sudden brainchild of a genius. It is the result of gradual improvement of an existing device, and has evolved because we have taken many people's ideas to solve known problems, such as needing separate devices for everything, phone size, and battery life.. And, it will continue to evolve.

Look around you. Is there something in your home that causes you frustration? How about the clutter of too many remote controls? Or, what about finding a convenient place in the kitchen to put your computer or tablet, which now holds all your recipes?

Think about what changes you might make to improve these frustrations.

ACTIVITY

TRASH TO TREASURE

A great way to increase idea generation is to look at common everyday items in a different way. Put into practice what you have learned about mind warping, getting more inputs, and being idea prone. This activity will help you practice these new skills.

1. Gather items from your junk drawer, closet, basement, and anywhere else you keep junk. Look for things you would sell at a garage sale or even just throw away. Some items I gathered for this exercise included old remote controls for VHS players I no longer

owned; 100 binder clips; paper clips; rubber bands; old CDs; keys that open who-knows-what; a deck of 45 playing cards; a picture frame without glass; ribbon; lace; and yarn.

2. After you have gathered your trash, lay it all out in front of you and consider what you can make out of it. Remember, to be creative it must solve a problem, such as a way to organize your child's jumbled Legos. Being aesthetically pleasing is a suitable if the problem is to fill a blank space on a wall or to add pizzazz to a sterile office.

3. Now it's time to get your glue, tape, staples, and nails and turn your idea into a treasure.

I made a windchime out of some of my items. With the remaining ones, I created a sci-fi-looking, robot creature that holds reminder notes. I named it Neville (Harry Potter fans will understand the joke).

Recognize Interconnections

"Creativity and insight almost always involve an experience of acute pattern recognition: the eureka moment in which we perceive the interconnection between disparate concepts or ideas to reveal something new."

– Jason Silva

"Vision without action is merely a dream. Action without vision just passes the time. Vision with action can change the world."

– Joel Barker

"Creative thought must always contain a random component."

– Gregory Bateson

"When you ask creative people how they did something, they feel a little guilty because they didn't really do it; they just saw something. It seemed obvious to them after a while."

– Steve Jobs

As the quotes suggest, it is the ability to SEE and ACT upon interconnections of unrelated things that define creative people. Often, they do not even know it is happening. It appears as if the muses whisper in their ears.

But the truth is that the moments of inspiration do not come from muses. They come from quickly drawing upon past experiences. There is a great documentary called "Everything is a Remix – The Elements of Creativity." It suggests that nothing is new, and everything created is a remix of something which has already been discovered.

According to its theory, you start by copying something that exists or an experience you had and then create something new from it. It's pretty spot on. When you look at the history of the greatest inventions or the greatest artists, their work is not completely original. It was neither invented nor created in a vacuum. There was something they saw or heard which provided inspiration and became the starting point. The inventor or artist then changed whatever it was that inspired them sufficiently so that it appeared to be a completely new and original idea. These are the interconnections in creativity.

Think of interconnections as the childhood game telephone. Do you remember playing it with a group of people? The first person starts by whispering something in the ear of the person next to her. The second person is to repeat the phrase to the third person. The third person repeats what he heard to the fourth person, and on and on down the line.

Then, at the end, the last person speaks the phrase out loud.

Usually, what the last person spoke was something funny and completely different from the original phrase.

This is similar to how creative interconnects work.

In this section, we will look at three ways you can use interconnections to create something new and unique.

1. Look to Nature—Biomimcry

As a creative person, I am always learning about new things. My current obsession is biomechanics, the study of the mechanics of biological systems. It has an interesting metamorphosis.

The industry of prosthetics was stuck in an archaic rut. I once heard someone say prosthetics were little more advanced than a pirate's peg leg. If you consider what artificial legs were like until recently, at the time this was an accurate statement. Back then, a prosthetic leg was nothing more than a solid plastic block with something that resembled a foot at the bottom, but engineers eventually began looking to add joints so that the foot could bend at the ankle. Then they analyzed how to make the prosthetics more comfortable. Today, prosthetics have become cutting edge.

This evolution didn't happen overnight, but once people started rethinking prosthetics, the entire industry began to change. Among the most talked about these days are the prosthetics developed for athletes. Instead of looking at the biomechanics of the human body, engineers look to nature.

For example, if a track athlete needs prosthetic legs, why not use the legs of the fastest animal on the planet? It didn't take long before we started seeing bilateral leg amputees running faster than most other people. Looking to nature to improve the prosthetics of athletes was a genius move!

The act of looking to nature to solve problems is call biomimicry. Let's look at a few more examples of how biomimicry can inspire creative ideas.

In 1941, George de Mestral was on a hunting trip in the Swiss Alps with his dog, an Irish Pointer. When he arrived home, his pants and the dog's fur were covered in burrs.

Instead of picking off the annoying pods, his curiosity (hint... curiosity = creativity) was piqued to understand how the burrs could stick to his dog's fur and his pant leg.

He studied the burr under a microscope and noticed that it was made of hundreds of tiny hooks.

Do you know where Mestral's discovery led? It led to the invention of Velcro. By mimicking the tiny hooks in the burrs and creating tiny loops of fabric, Mestral developed a new way to fasten clothing; an alternative to buttons, snaps, and zippers. And what kid doesn't want a pair of Velcro shoes so he doesn't have to deal with annoying laces that always come undone?

Need more proof that nature can provide creative solutions to problems?

NASA is currently trying to solve the problem of dealing with the cliffs on Mars. They've discovered it is not feasible for a robot to try to find a way around a cliff. This would waste valuable time and power, so they are looking for a biomimicry solution to help their robots climb the sheer cliffs.

One animal that may hold the solution is the gecko. Scientists are studying the gecko and how they climb sheer-faced surfaces. I would love to provide a simple answer to how they climb walls, but if it was simple, the NASA scientists would have already implemented the feature on the robots. So, let's just say to explain the phenomena it requires equations, math, and other high-tech science-stuff. If you are interested, search on Wikipedia for "gecko feet," It's fascinating though well over my head to completely understand.

What's important is that top NASA engineers and scientists recognize the importance of biomimicry as a way to solve problems in need of creative solutions. Are you now looking at your dog's fur and wondering what solutions to the world's biggest problems he may hold?

2. Unusual Connections—Bislocation

If you thought biomimicry was strange, imagine what you'll think about bislocation.

Bislocation is a term coined by author Arthur Koestler and means "to make a distinction between the routine skills of thinking on a single plane… and the creative act, which… always operates on more than one plane."

In more basic terms, bislocation is the act of putting two unrelated things together to make something new and useful. Examples of bislocation include how Christopher Sholes combined piano keys and letters to create the typewriter, or how by combining a pinecone and reading that Louise Braille created the braille system. Sholes and Braille each took two seemingly unrelated items and combined them to make something new and useful.

Making unusual connections is also used in comedy. I previously mentioned comedians are very creative, but some of their best and funniest work occurs when they unexpectedly join two known and unrelated elements to create something new.

The best demonstration of this is the comedy of Carrot Top. He is called the King of Prop Comedy. Carrot Top's jokes are based on trucks full of items he creates by putting two unrelated things together to make something that solves a problem—such as baby shoes with suction cups on the bottom, so your toddler can't run away from you.

Using bislocation can promote creative thinking.

Research from neuroscientists at the University of Bristol's Paul Howard-Jones has shown we think creatively when we are forced to find connections between different ideas. In one study, participants were asked to write a story based on three random words. Those participants given three unrelated words, such as fish, paper, and wheel, came up with more creative stories than the participants who were given more obviously associated words, like fish, water and bowl.

Creativity is sparked when we force our brain to find associations which are not obvious.

ACTIVITIES

1 ACTIVITY: BISLOCATION

1. Open any book to a random page.

2. Pick a random word.

3. Write it down.

4. Then, turn the page and pick another word.

5. Finally, turn to another page and select a third random word.

6. Now, set a timer for five minutes and write as many ways the three random words can be connected. You can also choose to write a story using the three words.

What did you come up with?

2 CARROT TOP ACT

1. Think of a problem, real or fictional.

2. Now, think of items you can put together to solve the problem. For example, a tea strainer and a glass of milk, so you no longer worry about losing your cookie when you dunk it.

What did you devise?

3. Make the Old New Again

Creating new things from something old is neither a surprising nor an original idea. We do it all the time. In his autobiography, actor, writer, and producer John Cleese advised, "Steal, steal an idea that you know is good, and try to reproduce it in a setting that you know and understand. It will become sufficiently different from the original because you are writing it, and by basing it on something good, you will be learning some of the rules… as you go along."

As the Monte Python alumnus suggested, do not be worried that by copying someone else's work or idea that you are not being creative. Here are a few techniques you can adapt to ensure the outcome is uniquely yours.

First, don't be afraid to break the rules. Sure, that's an old adage, but it is true. Just because something has always been done a specific way does not mean it is the only or right way to do it. Look at something and ask yourself how you can do it differently. Picasso, for example, broke the rules about what a woman's face should look like. Dick Fosbury changed the rules on how modern athletes complete the high jump when he decided to flop horizontally over the bar instead of jump vertically over it.

Next, play the "what if" game. There is no better way to discover creative improvements to products and processes than to ask, "What if?" Engineers and scientists do this all the time. They look at a product or process and ask questions aimed at finding ways to make improvements: "What if we sped up production?" "What if we made it bigger?" "What if we made it faster?" "What if we changed the order of the steps?" They have no preconceived notions. Rather, they ask questions and see where it leads them.

Finally, look to other industries for ideas. George Westinghouse got the idea for airbrakes while reading about a rock drill powered by an air compressor. Johannes Gutenberg saw the future development of the printing press when he looked at a wine press.

Ideas and inspiration are everywhere. Just open your eyes and look around.

ACTIVITY

COPYCAT

1. Choose an existing work of art or product (painting, appliance, storyline, machine, clothing, etc.) that you admire.

2. Set a timer for 15 minutes.

3. Brainstorm ways you can alter it and make it your own.

4. Then, select your favorite idea and implement it.

PREPARE YOUR EGO

ONE OF THE MOST DIFFICULT THINGS TO OVERCOME WITH CREATIVITY IS THE EGO. IT IS THE THING THAT STOPS US FROM TRYING SOMETHING DIFFERENT. WE ARE CONSTANTLY ASKING OURSELVES:

- What if we look foolish?
- What if we fail?
- What would other people say?

Ego is the thing that makes us think it is impossible. It screams:

- There is no way to complete that in such a short timeframe.
- That goal is too big.

It prevents us from using the strength of a team by warning:

- What if someone else takes the credit for my idea?
- Why are my ideas always skipped?
- What if they think I'm dumb?
- What if I'm stuck with someone dumb on my team?

When it comes to creativity, you need to set your ego aside. You must learn how to fail, deal with constraints, and work with others to optimize your creativity and produce your best ideas.

Fail… Like a Genius™

"Failure is the opportunity to begin again more intelligently."

– Henry Ford

"Creative achievement is the boldest initiative of the mind. An adventure that takes its hero simultaneously to the rim of knowledge and the limits of propriety."

– Robert Grandin

"When failure is not an option, we can forget about creativity, learning, and innovation."

– Brené Brown

"Creativity is making marvelous out of the discarded."

– Unknown

These quotes confirm that creativity and failure go hand-in-hand. When I set out to write this book, I thought this would be the easiest section. That's because there are so many great examples of failures turning into creative triumphs, and it is the one practice nearly all research agrees which leads to the road of innovation and success.

However, as I sit at my keyboard typing these words, I am facing my greatest dream and biggest fear. Ever since I was seven, I wanted to write a book and have it published. I have written dozens of stories over the years, but never finished any of them.

My excuses for this lack of follow-through are boundless: not enough time, I got a better idea, it wasn't going in the right direction, and on and on. But the truth is, I never finished a book because I was afraid of failing. I was afraid someone would tell me I suck as a writer and should give it up. Worse, I feared no one would ever want to read what I wrote.

Well, here I am, facing my internal monster, and since you are reading this, I must have slayed that dragon. (Yay me!)

Why should you care about the winged-beast that has scorched my dreams of writing for decades? Because I understand the struggles you go through when you have a great idea to fix a business problem but don't speak up during a meeting. I know what you feel when you spend months in the evenings designing a product that will revolutionize the grilling industry, but you never show anyone your blueprints.

We share the feeling of those choking claws of failure squeezing until you can barely breath. Together we recognize that as long as no one tells you the idea or the design or the manuscript is horrible, you can still daydream about the fairytale ending where you are declared a genius, are crowned with jewels, and the crowds in the streets shout your name in admiration. If you do not fail, you can pretend you will someday succeed.

Writing this book has proven to me this is crap. (I wish my computer had the smiling crap emoji, because that accurately illustrates that thinking.) It's a complete falsehood. If you never try, you will never succeed. Your dream will always remain exactly that—a dream. So how did I overcome my dragon, and what can you do to join me in this journey? I have a three-step method, which I named Fail… Like a Genius™.

1. **Embrace failure**
2. **Learn from failure**
3. **Reassess failure**

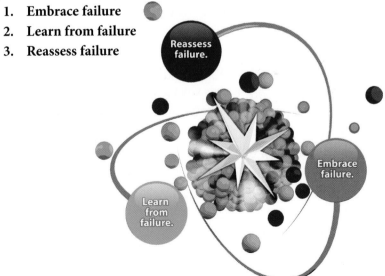

Fail … Like a Genius™

1. Embrace Failure

The first step of learning how to let go and develop your creativity is to put on your big girl or big boy pants and become comfortable with failure. Keep in mind, the people who judge you are also afraid of rejection. So, if the world does not shout your name in admiration, or if your boss does not implement your idea, it does not mean you suck and should give up. Rather, it simply means the idea was not right at that time or it needs to be adjusted.

Continue to dream and think of more ideas. Ask yourself: How can you modify your idea to make it work for the situation? What else can you try?

Thomas Edison is considered one of the greatest inventors in history. He failed all the time. What made him successful was that he did not give up when an experiment did not work. He implemented the best example of failing like a genius: he put a positive spin on it.

When asked about all his failed lightbulb experiments, Edison is reported to have said, "I have not failed. I've just found 10,000 ways that won't work."

He viewed each failure as an opportunity to learn something new and continue to move forward—creatively.

Yes, failure still seems scary. It's hard not to be a bit scared. Danielle Krysa, author of the book *Your Inner Critic is a Big Jerk*, offered a great idea for dealing with failure and the inner voice inside your head that tells you you're not good enough, worthy enough, or smart enough. Krysa says the next time the voice tries to paralyze you from speaking up during a meeting or sharing the next great American novel, give it a non-threatening name and tell it to shut up.

Let's call that inner voice Daisy.

How can you find Daisy threatening? What does Daisy know? Shut up Daisy!

Jerry Della Femina, a famous advertising man, said, "Failure is the mother of all creativity. My advice to anybody who wants to be creative is to get into something that will fail… Most people are afraid to fail, but once you've done it you find out it's not that terrible. There's a sense of freedom that you get from taking chances."

He's right. Once you embrace failure it can make you fearless.

This holds true even at some of the most prestigious organizations in the world. When combing through hundreds of resumes for future

ACTIVITY

FAILURE RESUME

1. To help you develop the thick-skin necessary to deal with the fear of failure, write a failure resume. Typically, when applying for a job, you write about your successes and all your former glory. You even stretch the truth a little appear more successful or more of an expert than you really are. But for this activity, look at your resume and rewrite it with all your failures.

2. List items such as:
   - What did not go right at the job?
   - Was there a time when you missed a deadline?
   - What about that time you got into an argument with a client?
   - Why did you wreck your company car?

Include your personal failures, such as not getting into the college of your choice, your divorce, the pipe which burst in your house and flooded everything because you forgot to shut off the water.

3. The final step of this activity is to share your resume with someone. (I think I just heard your scream of horror.) You do not have to share this resume with your employer. Instead, share it with a friend, significant other, or therapist; someone who probably already knows most of this information.

4. As you discuss your resume, talk about how you got past the failures. What steps did you take? Did any of the failures lead to successes? What lessons did you learn?

astronauts, NASA looks for evidence of some failure in the applicant's life. Things occasionally go wrong in space, and when they do it can mean life or death. NASA wants people who can get past these situations by thinking calmly and developing on-the-fly solutions.

2. Learn from Failure

How did the Failure Resume activity go? You survived, didn't you? The activity served two purposes: to help you become comfortable with failure, and to help you study and learn from mistakes. This is the second step to Fail… Like a Genius™.

Let's return to Thomas Edison.

Edison did not try only one method over and over 1,000 times to create an incandescent lightbulb until one finally worked. Instead, after each experiment failed, he studied what he did and the results. He then formulated a plan to improve or change his next experiment. Edison tweaked each approach. He tried to make the light last longer. Then he tweaked it to make it less expensive to produce and then he tweaked it more to reduce its size.

The lesson that Edison offers is that the only way a failure can turn into a success is to review why it failed and to try again in a different way. Sometimes, you need to adjust the materials, other times the process, and sometimes the purpose.

It is important to understand the difference between failure and being sloppy or lazy. If you have not given your best effort to a situation or problem, or if you continue to do the same thing over and over without success, you will continue to fail. Failing because you are sloppy or lazy is not excusable. That is why I say to fail… like a genius. Examine what did not go right. Correct it. And try again.

Sometimes the failure is that you are not sharing your idea with the right person or company. Failing like a genius involves getting past rejection, believing in your idea, and continuing forward until you find the right person willing to try it. There are endless stories about ideas that were rejected and would have been a failure had the person not forged ahead. For example, 12 publishers rejected J.K. Rowling's "Harry Potter and the Philosopher's Stone" before Bloomsbury picked it up for a paltry 1,500 pounds. The series went on to sell 450 million copies worldwide, but the only reason Harry Potter became the bestselling book series in history is because Rowling took those rejections as opportunities to improve the stories and try again with a different prospective publisher. She never lost faith and always believed her idea was good. Her relentless Failing... Like a Genius™ paid off.

The founder of KFC has a similar story. It took Colonel Harland David Sanders 1,009 tries before he found a restaurant that would sell his, now famous, secret chicken recipe.

3. Reassess Failure

Finally, the last step to Fail... Like a Genius™ is to reassess the failure and consider the possibility that your failure was not a failure.

Maybe your experiment did not produce the product or process you expected or wanted. Boo-hoo! Before you throw out your idea, consider if there is a different purpose for which it can be used. This happens all the time.

One of my favorite failure stories—and my favorite products—is from 3M. Dr. Spencer Silver, a 3M chemist, was working on a formula for a super-strong adhesive.

Unfortunately, his experiments yielded a weak adhesive which could stick to objects and be removed. At the time, this was a big failure.

However, one day, a colleague of Dr. Silver's became frustrated when trying to mark his place in his hymnal at church. He looked at his slips of paper and recalled the weak adhesive. The idea for Post-It® Notes was born. A failure became a huge success because a new purpose was found.

Another failure-turned-success is the story of Slinky.

The original idea was to develop a spring to support sensitive shipping equipment and keep it safe during voyages. The "wonderful thing" wasn't strong enough to support the heavy equipment, but it made a great toy and has since been sold to hundreds of millions of people.

TOOLBOX

FAIL... LIKE A GENIUS™ WORKSHEET
Follow this worksheet to fail like a genius.

Embrace failure
1. Identify who is judging you.
   a. If it is your inner critic:
      i. What is the name of your inner critic?
      ii. Read this sentence out loud: "Shut up [name of your inner critic]. You're a jerk. When you have something useful to say then I will listen."
   b. If it is someone else:
      i. Do you care what the critic says?
      ii. What personal fears might the critic have?
      iii. Never let them make you feel less of a person.
2. What is the worst thing that can happen?
   a. Does that matter? If so how can you mitigate that risk without giving up?
3. Do you have a support team you can talk to about your fears?

Learn from failure
1. What went wrong?
2. What went right?
3. How can the design or process be changed or adapted?
4. Is there helpful feedback in the criticism you can use to improve?
5. Is there someone with whom you can collaborate?
6. Was it the right audience? Is there someone else you should show?

Reassess failure
1. Can it be used for a different purpose?
2. Can it be combined with something to improve it?
3. How can you make it:
   a. Bigger or smaller
   b. Less expensive
   c. Last longer
   d. More versatile

Deal with Constraints

"Constraints can spur creativity and incite action, as long as you have the confidence to embrace them."

– Tom Kelley

"Constraints forces creativity."

– Jonathan Fields

"Creativity doesn't just love constraints; it thrives on them."

– David Burkus

Just as failure is an important part of creativity, so are constraints, as these quotes state. When defining creativity in the introduction of this book, I claimed for something to be creative it must solve a problem. Let's expand the definition by adding that this problem must also have constraints. The combination of problem and constraints create the need for a creative solution. Without both, a creative solution is less likely required or generated.

It is interesting that I often hear people say, "We didn't have time to be creative," or "The budget didn't allow for a creative solution." These constraints provide the best opportunity for our most brilliant, creative insights to emerge instead of letting ourselves fall back into the same old, band-aid solutions that did not previously solve the problem.

Constraints can take two forms: roadblocks or uncertainty. Here are some ways those constraints can become opportunities for creative solutions.

1. Detour Down the Path Less Traveled

A roadblock is an obstacle which prevents you from traveling a desired path. Typically, the path we've chosen is well-known, well-paved, and doesn't have many bumps or potholes. We also don't have to worry about low-hanging branches that might bang us on the head.

How boring!

Where's the fun and adventure?

Remember, to be creative we need to try new things and embrace new adventures. It is the same when faced with a roadblock.

Instead of looking at the roadblock as an annoyance, look at it as an opportunity to try something new and different. This is your chance to take a road less traveled, as Robert Frost would advise.

I regularly facilitate a workshop for instructional designers to help them add creativity to the training sessions they develop. During the workshop, I provide a scenario for the business problem. I have the participants work in groups to create a training plan to solve the problem.

During the first workshop, I did not want to hinder the participants' creativity, so I told them they had an unlimited budget and timeframe for developing the training.

What a mistake.

This was when I learned the importance of putting constraints on creativity.

The participants started at me, and the room fell completely silent for a few moments.

As the groups finally started to discuss solutions, I wandered around to listen to their conversations. I heard a few people mention they had no idea where to start. This was disconcerting.

When the groups started writing their training plans, I quickly noticed they were the same, boring training solutions the industry has overused for years. I was very disappointed. I thought the activity was a perfect way to really let these instructional designers stretch their creativity. I was wrong.

In a desperate move, I announced to the class that the client just called and changed the project parameters. I told them the problem has become critical and the client needs to implement the training as soon as possible. They now only have six weeks to develop and implement the training solution.

My original reasoning for this impromptu change was to make a few of the solutions I heard in groups impossible and to force them to think of other ideas, but what I didn't realize until after the exercise was over, was that it not only made some of the solutions impossible, it forced everyone to be more focused on the problem. They had to dig deep into their bag of tricks and alter their preconceived notions. The result was everything I had hoped for!

After the announcement of the changed timeline, instead of silence, my instructions were met with excited chatter. Everyone rushed to rethink their training solutions. Ideas flowed. Excitement was high. The creativity poured. You could feel the energy in the room.

Roadblocks help you become more creative by focusing your attention. If you have too many options, you fall back on known and boring solutions because you feel paralyzed. Having constraints forces you to choose a road less traveled. This is why some people feel they work better with a tight timeframe, and why procrastinators wait until the night before a deadline to finish a project.

Ernest Hemingway created writing challenges for himself to help him continuously improve and refine his writing. One challenge he set was to write a story using only six words. This forced him to choose his words carefully.

What did Hemingway devise? An amazingly powerful and emotional story:

"For sale: baby shoes, never worn."

ACTIVITIES

1 **ASPEN VACATION**

Imagine you are vacationing at a ski resort in Aspen. Write a postcard about your vacation, but do not use the words "snow" or "cold."

2 **ONE THING**

1. Set a timer for 5 minutes.

2. Write a slogan or jingle for the company where you work.

3. Next, reset the timer for 5 minutes.

4. Write another slogan or jingle, but this time you must include the word "blush."

Which exercise was more difficult—with or without the constraints? And, which of the two slogans or jingles is most creative?

2. Reimagine Your Environment

When people are presented with a problem, they often assume constraints which do not exist. For example, you may assume there is a low budget when specific numbers were not discussed for a project.

People also often assume things must be used in the manner for which they were originally designed to be used. The best way to illustrate this misconception is with a story.

Most people know about Apollo 13, the mission to the moon that turned into a rescue mission. One of the best stories of turning roadblocks into a creative solution was when the engineers had to figure out how to make a square filter fit into a round opening so the astronauts could get fresh oxygen and filter out carbon dioxide. They literally had to figure out how to fit a square peg into a round hole. The constraints were that they could only use items the astronauts had onboard, and the procedures had to be something the astronauts could replicate in space.

My favorite part of the movie was when mission control instructed the astronauts to tear off the front cover of the flight manual. I loved it—first, because I write manuals and I have a healthy sense of humor about what people think of technical manuals. Secondly, I loved this part because it demonstrated how sometimes, to overcome roadblocks, you need to look at your available resources in a different way. You must learn to use things in ways they were not originally intended to be used. This requires rethinking the purpose of everything around you.

In my workshops, I conduct an activity inspired by the Apollo 13 story. Groups are provided with a gallon-sized Ziplock® bag which contains several items. Then, I tell them this story: While on a five-day hiking trip, the lid on my water bottle broke. It is important to carry water, and carrying it without a lid would be difficult.

The groups are given the bags and told this is everything I decided I could spare from my backpack. They are then instructed to find a way for me to carry water so it does not spill, so I can easily drink from it, and so I can refill it.

Most groups restrict their solutions to only the items inside the plastic bag. However, the groups that create the workable solutions incorporate the bag.

The very best solutions have come from groups that not only used the bag, but also disassembled the Chapstick and used the hollow tube and cap from it to create a new lid.

The lesson is this: Do not assume constraints which do not exist, and always look at how you can use things in alternate ways.

Remember the story of Pixar I mentioned in Part One? The company's management team had the creative idea to make money by marketing their computer to other industries besides animation. They realized the medical field would have an interest in 3D imagining, and this decision provided the cash flow necessary to grow and expand the business.

Another example is what people have done with drones. Look at all the creative ways they are being used, such as to replant acres of rain forest that have suffered from deforestation. This application is not only creative but it saves time and money because drones can easily get into places which are too difficult for trucks to reach.

ACTIVITIES

1 BLACKOUT

Artist and writer Austin Kleon is known for creating poems by using the writing of someone else and blacking out words. The words that remain on the page form Kleon's poem.

Try to write a poem like Kleon.

1. Take a page from a magazine, newspaper, or book.

2. Use a black marker to block out the words you do not want to use. The words left on the page should create your poem.

2 PAPER

How many ways can you think to use a binder clip?

1. Make a list of ideas on a sheet of paper.

2. When you're finished, type "uses for binder clips" into a search engine.

How did you do? Did you have any ideas that did not appear in your search?

Learn to Use Collaboration and Competition

"We all need people who give us feedback. That's how we improve."

– Bill Gates

"For all good ideas and true innovation, you need human interaction, conflict, argument, debate."

– Margaret Heffernan

"Unity is strength… when there is team work and collaboration wonderful things can be achieved."

– Mattie Stepanek

"Competition is a by-product of productive work, not its goal. A creative man is motivated by the desire to achieve, not by the desire to beat others."

– Ayn Rand

Great ideas happen when great minds work together or against each other as these quotes state. Learning to use collaboration and competition in creative thinking can often be the most difficult for one's ego. But why do we fear working with others?

Yes, it is fear. Do not kid yourself into thinking the root cause is anything else. We fear collaborating because we fear being judged, and we fear having our ideas stolen by others.

Competition comes with other baggage: it causes stress, pressure, and sometimes brings out the worst in people.

While on the surface these don't sound beneficial to creative thinking, they are. However, when entering into a collaboration or competition to solve a problem it is good to set a few ground rules.

First, create a safe environment. Everyone should understand that they can share creative ideas without judgment or ridicule. If someone cannot follow the rules, they should be dismissed. These people quickly become a hinderance to finding a solution. Working in a safe, collaborative or competitive environment leads to more optimism, excitement, and possibilities. It produces a better mindset, more realistic solutions, and feelings of connectedness. Collaboration leads to greater tribal knowledge and provides more experiences from which to draw ideas.

Even if your creative group is you and one other person, there are benefits. It helps you keep each other's energy high and balance the way each of you think and work.

Joshua Wolf Shenk, author of *Powers of Two: Seeking the Essence of Innovation in Creative Pairs*, explains the power of collaboration and competition in creativity and innovation by offering a reminder of a few powerful competitors and collaborators: "Competition and collaboration are often intertwined. Only when we explore this terrain can we grasp how such pairs as Steve Jobs and Steve Wozniak, William and Dorothy Wordsworth, and Martin Luther King Jr. and Ralph Abernathy all managed to do such creative work. The essence of their achievements... was relational."

Comedy improv—yes, this makes another appearance in creativity thinking—has a rule of its own: "yes and..."

The rule outlines that when you are presented with something, you accept it. You go with it, do not contradict it, and then add to it. For example, your partner on stage holds up a skein of yarn and says, "This used to be my dog."

If you contradict her statement, it ruins the comedy.

Instead, you say something like, "Yes, and now that he's dead, he's become my mop."

This technique requires collaboration with your partner on stage. There is also a little bit of competition because each comedian wants to be the funniest.

When you work with a group of people, consider using the "yes and..." rule. It will help everyone avoid judging ideas, and make them feel all ideas are being heard and considered. Take what is said and modify it. Others will catch on and do the same. This is the foundation of active brainstorming.

ACTIVITY

INFOMERCIAL

This is a group activity.

1. Choose a nearby object. It should be something that you can hold in your hand.

2. Pretend you are an expert on this object. You've spent your entire life studying it and its kind. No one knows more about this object than you do.

3. For the next 60 seconds, state everything you know about the object. The goal is to prove in one minute that you are an expert on your object.

Talk for the entire 60 seconds. Don't pause to think or judge.
Speak out loud.

4. Now pass the object to someone.

They must incorporate the "yes and..." rule and continue to talk about the object as if they are another expert. They may provide evidence of what you said as truth or they may offer new uses for the object.

QUICK HITS TO FLIP THE CREATIVITY SWITCH

PART V

SO, YOU'VE MADE IT THIS FAR. CONGRATULATIONS! YOUR REWARD IS A COLLECTION OF QUICK INSPIRATIONS AND ACTIVITIES WHICH YOU CAN REFER TO WHEN YOU NEED TO GET YOUR CREATIVE JUICES FLOWING.

Inspirations
Here are some places where you can turn or things you can do to find inspiration that helps your creativity.

1. Advice from Experts
The following are tidbits from extremely creative people on how to be creative and generate more ideas.

Christoph Niemann, Illustrator. He describes creativity as:
- 87 percent effort—working or thinking hard about the problem
- 7.5 percent luck
- 0.5 percent talents or divine inspiration
- 5 percent staying off the Internet for consecutive 90 minutes. (This is a joke, but also true. You must guard against "time suck" distractions that pepper the landscape of everyday events. Don't multitask!)

Elizabeth Gilbert, author of *Eat, Pray, Love.*

- Guard your time set aside for creating.
- Learn how to say "no" to things you want to do.
- Ask yourself: What are you willing to give up?
- Sometimes, the worst place you can be is in a room with a lot of other creatives, especially when you are trying to find your creative voice.
- The best thing you can do is to go out and have a lot of experiences.
- Sometimes, you get ideas through research.
- Don't be afraid if through the creative process your idea goes in a different direction than you originally intended.
- Don't be afraid to create just for the sake of creativity. It doesn't always have to have a purpose. Just the act of creating can help to further inspire you and renew your creativity.

Bruce Nussbaum, professor of Innovation and Design, Parsons, The New School of Design, adds these definitions:

- Knowledge Mining: Connecting information from a variety of sources in new ways
- Framing: Understanding how your point of view differs from and compares to other people's.
- Playing: The ability to explore risk and possibility in the context of a game.
- Making: The desire and ability to create something tangible.
- Pivoting: The ability to transition quickly between concepts and production.

Danielle Krysa, author of *Your Inner Critic is a Big Jerk*

- Copy the experts
- Always work on your creative passion
- Give space and time to be creative. If you have time to be on Facebook, you have time to be creative
- Trust yourself

- Give your inner critic a new name. It should be something non-threatening. It's easier to tell it to shut up if it can't be helpful.
- Say "Thank you." Don't point out your flaws when someone compliments you.
- Accept that things don't have to be perfect. Use scratch paper for jotting down ideas as fast as you can. Then, put them on "good paper." Many people fear writing on a clean page.
- Translate and rewrite. If your inner critic says that you will embarrass yourself if you continue, rewrite it to "I am going to have fun and laugh with the audience. We are going to have fun and learn a lot."

2. Standup and Stretch

Get out of your chair and give your butt a rest!

- Standup. Reach your arms over your head. Reach as high as you can. As you are stretching, take deep and slow breathes.
- Lean to the right. Then lean to the left.
- Reach your arms in front of you as far as you can. Clasp your hands behind your back and lift them up.
- Turn your head as far to the right as you can; then turn it to the left.
- Roll your shoulders back five times and then roll them to the front.
- Shake your body loose.

3. Look on the Internet

If you need inspiration, try doing a search using Google images. I use it for topics for my daily writing prompts.

Pinterest is another excellent site for inspiration. You can find ideas about everything.

There are also numerous idea generators available online. Writers use them for character names, location descriptions, and even plot twists.

4. Mind Map or Draw a Picture

Sometimes, you just need to change things up. When working out a problem, drawing a picture of it or creating a mind map may help you find a solution. Either approach allows you to look at the problem through a new lens.

5. Exercise

Do a few jumping jacks to get your blood flowing and to clear your mind. Take a walk around the block to step away from the problem you are trying to solve.

6. Meditate and Breathe

Bring down your stress level and get your mind creating serotonin by taking deep breathes or meditating.

Find a quiet place.

Get comfortable.

Close your eyes.

Now, concentrate on inhaling and exhaling.

Continue doing this until you feel more relaxed and your mind is clear.

7. Memory or Vision Boards

A memory board is designed to hold items which remind you of inspirational things or experiences you've had. A vision board contains items which remind you of goals you want to achieve.

Make a memory or vision board. It will keep inspiration or a goal at the center of your focus. You can search "How to make a vision board DIY" on Pinterest for ideas on how to make one.

A memory or vision board that shows multiple pieces of inspirational material together can help spark ideas and create connections between objects whenever you need them most.

8. Share

Sharing your ideas has several of benefits:

- Personal accountability

- An audience can help keep you motivated to continue working
- It is difficult to stop if others are watching
- Create a feedback loop
  - Others can help lead you in the right direction
  - Ditch the ego and you will see how others have invaluable insight
- Grow an invested community
  - When people care what you are doing, it energizes you
  - Communities make you feel what you are doing is valuable

ACTIVITY

Here are some activities to kick start your mind into creative thinking.

1 A BIT OF EVERYTHING ACTIVITY

This combines several techniques you learned throughout the book, such as warping your mind, not overthinking, bislocation, and dealing with constraints.

1. Divide a piece of paper into four quadrants.

2. At the bottom of the first quadrant, write the word "nature."

3. At the bottom of the second quadrant, write the word "freedom."

4. At the bottom of the third quadrant, write the word "fear."

5. Finally, at the bottom of the fourth quadrant, write the word "euphoria."

6. Set a timer for 15 minutes.

7. Draw a picture representing each of these words, but there are constraints... or opportunities. Your picture can only consist of four straight lines and one circle for each word. You do not have to use all the lines and the circle, but you cannot use more than four lines and one circle to draw a picture representing each word.

ACTIVITY

2 20 CIRCLES ACTIVITY

As described earlier in the book, for this activity, you need to photocopy the following page of circles create your own on a piece of paper. If you opt to create your own, draw 20 circles approximately 1 ½" in diameter on the paper. Use additional pieces of paper if necessary to reach 20 circles.

You also need a writing instrument—a pencil, pen, marker, etc.—and a timer.

1. Set the timer for three minutes.

2. Within those three minutes, draw inside each circle to turn it into something different. For example, turn the first circle into a smiley face and the second into a baseball. Do this with as many of the circles as you can—creating different objects for each circle. Do not duplicate.

3. At the end of three minutes, count how many circles you completed. Did you transform all 20 circles? If not, that is OK. It takes practice to generate ideas. Take a break and try again.

How did you do this time?

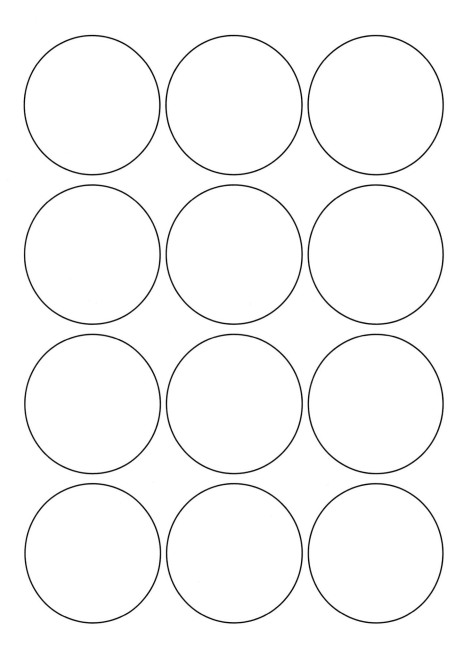

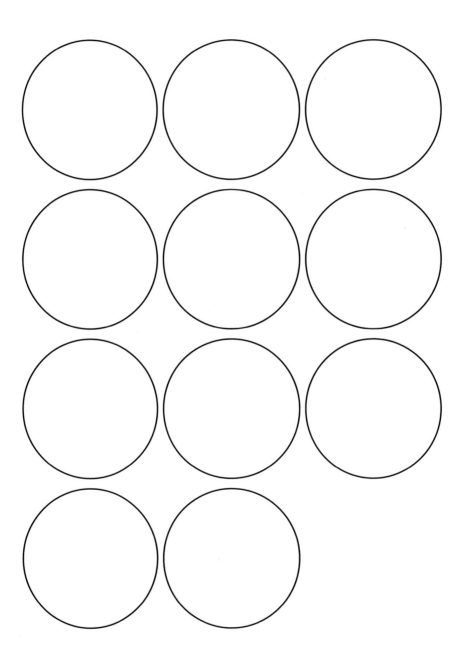

ACTIVITY

3 HEIGHT CHALLENGE

1. Pretend you are four feet tall. Write what your daily routine looks like.

2. As you go through your daily routine, what things are difficult to accomplish? How would you change your environment to accommodate your height to make your daily routine easier?

3. Do the same thing, but now imagine you are seven feet tall.

4. Select one problem you discovered and brainstorm ideas to solve the problem. What steps would be required to develop one of your solutions? What resources would you need? Is it something that could be marketed?

TOOLBOX

Here are some tools you can add to your personal toolbox which will assist you with creative thinking when you most need them.

1 Be Prepared

Once you train yourself to be creative and to be idea prone, it is important to ensure you are always prepared to capture the ideas as they arise. How many times have you had a great idea only to forget what it was later? Here is what you need to keep on hand to stop that from happening:

- **Mini notepad and pen.** Use something that will fit in a purse, computer bag, pocket, or glove compartment... as well as neatly in your hand. I have several notebooks scattered around my house and office so one is always available when I need it.
- **Dry erase marker.** This was an idea I saw in a YouTube video. The man said he always got his best ideas in the shower, but he would forget the idea by the time he left the bathroom. So, he kept a dry erase marker in the bathroom. This way, he could capture his idea on the mirror. Later, he would transfer the idea to his notebook and then easily erase the marker from the mirror.
- **Notepad, pen, and low-watt light.** This is something you should keep next to your bed. Often, we get great ideas just before falling asleep or in the middle of the night. We don't capture those ideas because we rarely want to get up and look for something to write with. Having the notepad and pen by the bed means you do not have to search. The low-watt light helps from hurting your eyes or waking up anyone else.
- **Whiteboard or corkboard.** Sometimes, you'll get a great idea but you aren't ready to act on it. Putting the idea on a whiteboard or corkboard keeps the idea in front of you so you do not forget about it, and it preserves it so that you can revisit the idea when you are ready.

TOOLBOX

2 **HAND TOYS AND WAKE-UP BAGS™**
Here's how I made them:

INSTRUCTIONS

1. **Purchase material in bright colors.** I bought four fat-quarters (pre-cut material measuring 18" x 22"), which was enough to make 54 bags.

2. **Purchase coffee beans.** You don't need to buy the expensive stuff. The cheaper beans have just as strong of an aroma. I bought a 2lb bag of hazelnut flavored beans and had plenty leftover.

3. **Cut the material into 3" x 3" squares.** I'm a quilter so I have the fancy cutting board and rotary cutter already available. If you don't have these items, use a ruler and pen to mark the WRONG side of the fabric in 3" x 3" squares and the cut the material using scissors. (The WRONG side of the fabric is the side that you don't see when you are done. Typically, it is lighter in color than the RIGHT side of the fabric, which is the side you see when done.)

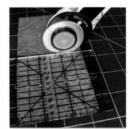

Step 3:
Cut to 3" x 3"

4. **Put two of the squares together with RIGHT sides facing each other and pin them in the center.** This keeps them from moving while you sew.

continued on page 130

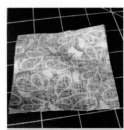

Step 4: Pin RIGHT sides together

TOOLBOX

HAND TOYS AND WAKE-UP BAGS™
continued from page 129

5. Stitch along three sides of the square.

6. **Stitch on the fourth side so that there is a 1" opening in the center.** This is how you will turn the material RIGHT side facing out and fill the bag with beans.

Steps 5 & 6: *Stitch leaving 1" opening*

7. **Snip all four corners being careful not to cut inside the stitches.** This makes your corners pointed instead of rounded.

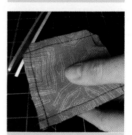

Step 7: *Trim corners*

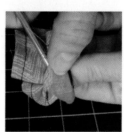

Step 8: *Turn RIGHT side out*

8. **Turn the bags RIGHT side facing out.** I use a crochet hook to help since the opening is small.

9. **Use a funnel to fill the bag with beans.** I made a funnel out of cardboard stock and used between one and two tablespoons of beans to fill the bags. Don't overstuff them. You want them squishy.

Step 9: *Fill with coffee beans*

10. Use a needle and coordinating thread to stitch the bag closed.

11. Your Wake-up Bag™ is ready for whenever you need a little creative boost.

Step 10: Hand-stitch closed

TOOLBOX

3 **POST-IT® NOTES**

Post-It® Notes are a great way to capture an idea or problem and then to expand it. Each Post-It® should have a different idea.

Place them on a wall or table. It is easy to move them around into different groups or steps. Post-Its are great to use when brainstorming.

4 **IDEA JOURNAL**

This is where you will write all your ideas. Don't try to remember your ideas, because you will forget. The idea journal can be a notebook or recorder. If you get an idea, but don't have your journal write the idea down on paper and put it in your journal later. Periodically review your idea journal for ideas to implement or ideas that inspire you.

INVITATION

Jennifer Yaros is a speaker, consultant, and coach who has a passion for guiding individuals and organizations through the exciting journey of creative and innovative success. Interested in having Jennifer facilitate a creativity or innovation workshop or discussion at your organization? You can reach her at:

Website: www.brainspark-creativity.com
Email: jyaros@radcomservices.com
LinkedIn: JenniferYaros
Facebook: JenniferYaros, BrainSpark
Twitter: @JenniferYaros